# Edward Bellamy Speaks Again!

*A volume in the Hyperion reprint series*

**THE RADICAL TRADITION IN AMERICA**

HX86
B43
1975

**HYPERION PRESS, INC.**
*Westport, Connecticut*

*"Ill fares the land, to hastening ills the prey,
Where wealth accumulates, and men decay."*

Oliver Goldsmith

Edward Bellamy

# Edward Bellamy Speaks Again!

## Articles—Public Addresses—Letters

*"For we brought nothing into this world, and it is certain we can carry nothing out."*

I. Tim. 6:7

1937

## THE PEERAGE PRESS

### Kansas City, Missouri

Published in 1937 by The Peerage Press, Kansas City
Copyright 1937 by The Peerage Press
Hyperion reprint edition 1975
Library of Congress Catalog Number 75-302
ISBN 0-88355-207-8
Printed in the United States of America


Library of Congress Cataloging in Publication Data

Bellamy, Edward,  1850-1898.
  Edward Bellamy speaks again!

  (The Radical tradition in America)
  Reprint of the ed. published by Peerage Press,
Kansas City, Mo.
    1. Government ownership--Addresses, essays,
lectures.  2. Socialism--Addresses, essays, lectures.
I.  Title.
HX86.B43     1975        335          75-302
ISBN 0-88355-207-8

# TABLE OF CONTENTS

# TABLE OF CONTENTS—(*Continued*)

# Foreword

*"The crest and crowning of all good.*
*Life's final star, is Brotherhood,*
* * * * *: * * * * * *

*And till it come, we men are slaves*
*And travel downward to our graves."*
—Edwin Markham.

IT WAS in the latter part of the last century that the star of Edward Bellamy flashed across the literary sky of America and left an impression that is deep and permanent. It was apparently his unique mission to so dramatize the age-old economic problem as to set people thinking along those lines who had never thought before. He succeeded. In these modern days we need no urge, we are compelled to think. The economic problems Bellamy visioned in his time and whose increasing gravity he so clearly forecast, are pressing now for solution with an insistence that will not be denied.

On that account the matter presented in the current volume should be of interest. It consists of Bellamy material never before brought together in volume form. Public addresses, articles that appeared in the periodicals of his day, letters: all reveal the same keenly analytical mind and the same lover of his fellow men. Reproduced as originally published, allowance should be made for any slight discrepancies in orthography or arrangement

9

# FOREWORD

attributable to the fact that the matter first appeared nearly a half century ago, one article at least having been written for publication in England for English readers.

His powerful novel, "Looking Backward," was first published in 1888. In it he gave an attractive and prophetic picture of American civilization in the year 2000, indicating also the methods by which it had been brought about. It gave him enduring fame. Much water has passed under the bridge since then. Noting national and world conditions today however, also the comparative rapidity of evolutionary change, it is not improbable that the fame he acquired in the past may be far exceeded by the fame that will be his in the years to come. This, because the remarkable clarity and finality of his thinking is today being demonstrated by the thunderous chorus of events, while the correctness of his conclusions as to program and method—by most considered fantastic at the time—seem after fifty years quite natural if not inevitable. Moreover, we still have over sixty years to go.

We are witnessing today a world in singular unrest. Here in our own country we are still facing unsolved problems of major importance after several years of sincere effort to find workable solutions. Conditions have been ameliorated but basic causes have not been removed. The best we have been able to do is to attempt a cure by the application of outworn principles. As a nation, we fail to see or dislike to admit that it is the logical result of dependence upon these same principles in the past that has brought us where we are. Our approach to normal activity in many leading industries of

# FOREWORD

the country, while a relief and satisfaction to those ac-
tually participating, is accompanied by the spectacle of
many millions still without employment or any immediate
prospect of worth while work to do.

The logical consequences arising from the operation
of a competitive economy with which we are struggling
are driving many to the conclusion that there can be no
security for the individual, under it. It is becoming evident that security for each can be attained only by providing for the security of all. We have good reason to
believe that our production facilities are adequate to provide a measure of average well-being never before ap-
proached, but to avail ourselves of such potential abundance, narrow self-interest will have to give way to some
all-embracing social plan designed for the equal benefit
of every citizen.

Some day, and the day may not be far off, we may
be willing to turn to the plans and specifications for the
building of such a democratic nation as has been outlined by Edward Bellamy. In the meantime, America
and the world owe him much for his courageous thinking and for his clear exposition of the logical content
of the democratic idea.

Bellamy was not the friend of any particular class of
men only, he was the friend of all men. A clear-reason-
ing, keenly intelligent, far-seeing believer in democracy,
he made a powerful plea for its complete fulfillment. He
has influenced millions in this and other countries
through his writings and is never forgotten by those who
read his two books: "Looking Backward" and "Equality" with serious intent. The former is said to have

11

enjoyed the greatest sale of any book published in America up to its time with the exception of "Uncle Tom's Cabin." The second, published ten years later, was an amplification of the original theme and an answer to questions raised by the former. They have both been translated into many languages and "Looking Backward" has been reproduced in Braille.

In the early nineties, as a result of the popularity of "Looking Backward" and the interest in a new order it created, there grew up in the country what was known as the Nationalist movement. It was devoted to the promulgation of economic reform along the lines indicated by Mr. Bellamy in his famous book. It had its own periodicals: "The Nationalist" and "The New Nation," and drew to its support many who were widely known in the progressive thought of the day. No educational movement of its magnitude could fail to wield an enduring influence even though the time was not ripe for the completion of its program.

The word "Nationalism," prominent in this collection and as used by Bellamy adherents over forty years ago, should not be confused with the foreign political use of the term today. The Bellamy conception of Nationalism was wholly in harmony with his theory of a democratic state and was adopted as an appropriate name for a movement furthering such an ideal. It is desirable that this be clearly understood. To that end the reader will find included in the volume an interesting article under the title: "Why the Name Nationalism?" written by one of the early Nationalists. It is introduced to make clear the origin and scope of the word as applied to the Na-

12

tionalist movement of the Nineties, which in turn received its impetus from the wide circulation of "Looking Backward."

For the benefit of those who may be unacquainted with the fact, Bellamy was first and foremost, the advocate of gradual and orderly change in his program of Nationalism. He also insisted that the decision to enter upon such an extension of function must be arrived at by democratic processes. His long study of the factors involved had convinced him that successful economic modifications must be predicated upon education and understanding. Every step taken must be justified by results and no good thing displaced until it could be superseded by something better. To such a method of advance, the soul of moderation and reasonableness, all believers in the democratic process should be able to subscribe.

It is an interesting fact that Bellamy forecast many of the conveniences and mechanical advancements that have become commonplace accessories of our everyday life, including the radio. These evidences of an almost uncanny prescience fifty years ago may possibly indicate that he has just as accurately forecast the character of the social changes that are inevitable in our evolving civilization. Be that as it may, the spirit that characterizes the Bellamy approach to the economic problems that confront us, is the spirit that should prevail whatever the details of procedure or the program advocated.

In reality there is nothing wholly new or startling in the plan he proposed as the framework of a nation responsive to the needs of its people. He regarded it as the essence of plain, common sense. From the beginning

13

of modern industry there has been a constant growth in the size and scope of business organizations. The company or corporation, the trust, the holding company—devices for the grouping of capital and for its management and control—have grown into use as the need became apparent under our profit economy, until we now have business aggregations whose fields are international and some whose monopoly in our own country is practically complete.

Bellamy noted the development of the corporation in his day and pointed out that the time would come when it would be necessary to decide whether concentrated ownership and control in private hands should be permanent, or whether the nation as a whole would be compelled in self-protection to carry the concentration process on to a logical conclusion, operating ultimately the great plant of organized national industry for all the people concerned. The first supposition spelled plutocracy. The second meant the triumph of democracy. The acceptance of the first meant loss of liberty for the masses, growing restriction of opportunity, the sinking of a whole population into virtual slavery. The adoption of the other meant the safeguarding of hard-won liberties, the independence in harmony with cooperative enterprise, the equalization of social benefits.

Edward Bellamy remarked that the millionaire and the tramp appeared upon the American scene at the same time. If he were here today he would probably point out that reputed billionaires and millions out of employment seem also to be coincident in the development of our industrial life. In a favored land, with natural re-

14

sources unequalled, we have apparently reached a point where an uncomfortably large percentage of our population has been set aside as no longer necessary in the operation of our industrial règime. They are now privileged to stand on the sidelines and watch the procession of fractional prosperity go by, leaving them behind. It is therefore quite understandable that we begin to hear more and more of correlated national industry. It is not intended to belittle the unprecedented efforts that have been put forth to remedy the condition referred to. It is perhaps the best we can do in the present state of national consciousness. It is not the best we could do if we could free ourselves from prejudice, tradition and a general feeling of personal irresponsibility.

Bellamy advocated the actual incorporation of a live-and-let-live principle in social organization. By many his proposed economic structure is regarded as idealistic, something impossible of attainment. He dared to prophesy a bright future for the nation based upon the actual realization of complete democracy. He called it the "Republic of the Golden Rule," nothing less than a recognition of the fact that the Sermon on the Mount embodied principles that are of universal application—the ultimate in wisdom and practicality. We will have to grow to perfect it, but if it be impractical in the long run, what of a world still exhibiting the extremes of wealth and poverty, now arming to the teeth, as an illustration of the success of an economic order accepted and supported by supposed practical men?

We profess to believe in the desirability of harmony in our lives and surroundings. We desire harmony between neighbors, between races, between nations. Harmony is the result of the absence of seriously conflicting interests. Logically it should follow that harmony in our own nation would be furthered by consummating an identity of interest in the means whereby we all live. Mr. Bellamy is convinced that national harmony will be attained in the degree that we approach the goal of co-operative effort in the production and distribution of wealth. Once the goal is reached the interest of one would be the interest of all. National policy would automatically benefit all or work injury to all. Its correction in the latter case would, theoretically, be prompt and effective. It would constitute a national demonstration of the maxim: "In union there is strength," also of its corollary: "United we stand, divided we fall." In our present competitive order it is obvious that private interests continually conflict and can hardly do otherwise except as they combine in certain areas to present a common front to other interests with which they continue to conflict.

One thing is reasonably certain: we have wandered in the economic wilderness of contrasted lack and plenty long enough if there is a practical way out. With present-day advances in science coupled with the continued development of labor-saving machinery, we are surely within sight at least of the abundance of the promised land. It may take many years for us to perfect social arrangements that will enable us to reach it, but the important thing is that we realize the goal and make a conscious start.

There are those who fear the coming of fascism and

yet another class who profess to see the possibility of communism in these United States. It should be unnecessary for us to experience either of these developments in America, still the stronghold of democracy. The national plan of Edward Bellamy outlined in this collection and given concrete treatment in his famous books: "Looking Backward" and "Equality," is no dream or fanciful tale of an impossible felicity. Moreover, his devastating appraisal of our present economic arrangements is difficult to refute. Bellamy argues for the middle way. He is not the advocate of a class movement, but for a democratic organization of society as broad as humanity, doing away with classes and making impossible the existence of a single forgotten man.

We suffer from fear, inertia and delusions. One of the latter is that the Golden Rule is an idealistic conception that can be set aside in the formulation of industrial programs. We seem not to dare to believe collectively many things that we believe personally and privately. We condone cruelties that are remediable and tolerate maladjustments in society that defy the most ordinary common sense. We are cowed by custom and browbeaten by habit. We are prone to worship the idea of possession rather than the ability to produce. We judge others quite generally by a deceptive money standard instead of by their usefulness to society through their vision or creative ability. We cling to the belief that our problems are individual problems when a growing but undetermined percentage are clearly bound up with the community life we seem destined henceforth to live. We seek to rely upon the undisputed virtues of rugged indi-

17

# FOREWORD

vidualism as a sufficient panacea for our ills in a world become so small and closely knit together that we can fly around it. We acknowledge the necessity for the care of social casualties after they occur, but are slow to understand and eliminate their cause. Still, we are learning by experience and have learned much in the past few disillusioning years though our tuition has come high.

An increasing number are coming to believe that near the end of the last century Edward Bellamy made an epochal contribution to the problem of creating a secure and happy America for ALL its people in the fateful years ahead. Those who read the new volume: "Edward Bellamy Speaks Again," and have not read his books heretofore mentioned in which he gives in detail his conception of man's relationship to the social order, have an interesting experience in store coupled with a liberal education in the humanities. Read Bellamy! Once thoughtfully read and pondered, he is capable of giving the reader new eyes to see with, new ears to hear with and a new mind and heart with which to understand and interpret this world in which we live.

R. Lester McBride,

*Pasadena, California*
*August, 1937*

# Edward Bellamy

*(From The American Fabian—June, 1898)*

IT IS doubtful if any man, in his own lifetime, ever exerted so great an influence upon the social beliefs of his fellow-beings as did Edward Bellamy. Marx, at the time of his death, had won but slight recognition from the mass; and though his influence in the progressive struggle has become paramount, it is through his interpreters, and not in his own voice, that he speaks to the multitude. But Bellamy spoke simply and directly; his imagination conceived, and his art pictured, the social framework of the future in such clear and bold outlines that the commonest mind could understand and appreciate. Wherever, in all lands, men are striving for a fairer social order based upon an economic democracy, Bellamy is a recognized prophet of the ideal state.

He was born at Chicopee Falls, Mass., March 28, 1850, and was the son of a Baptist minister. After a partial course at Union College he studied for a time in Germany. Returning home, he studied law and was admitted to the bar at Springfield. He disliked the profession, and did not begin practice, but instead engaged in newspaper work. He was a member of the staff of the New York "Evening Post" during a part of the years 1871-72, and for the next five years was an editorial writer and critic on the Springfield "Union." His health failing, he spent most of the year 1877 in the Hawaiian

Islands. On his return in 1878 he published his first novel, "A Nantucket Idyl." "Dr. Heidenhoff's Process," appeared in 1880. The same year he joined his brother, Charles J., in beginning the publication of the Springfield "News." His third novel, "Miss Ludington's Sister," appeared in 1884. "Looking Backward" was published early in 1888. In 1891 he started the "New Nation," which had for a time a considerable success, but ran out in 1893. After the publication of "Equality," May, 1897, indications of consumption appeared, and his physician advised him to go to Colorado. He went there in September, but failing to rally, returned home in April. He died in the early morning of May 22.

Bellamy's conversion to Socialism came to him in the course of his writing "Looking Backward." The sight of German and Swiss festivals in honor of war prompted him to begin a story celebrating the victories of peace. The picture of an ideal social state came to him piecemeal, was slowly put together, and from the contact of his vivid imagination with the dry facts of social statics came the peace, order and beneficence of the society depicted in his epoch-making novel. From the hour when the new order in its fullness dawned on him he was no longer the writer of fiction, but the prophet and revealer of a new dispensation. His energies were given unhesitatingly to the work of propagating the faith. He sought to permeate with his doctrines the liberal movements throughout the country; he was often in attendance at conventions and gatherings of reformers of differing creeds, seeking to win from them a recognition of a part at least of the truth of Nationalism; and it is to him that

EDWARD BELLAMY

is due much of the credit for the strong collectivist tone
of the Omaha platform of 1892. He encouraged the
work of THE AMERICAN FABIAN, and shortly before his death had interested himself in the revival of
the "New Nation."

There is and will continue to be great disparity of view
as to his rank among the world's reformers. Some of
the philistine journals have spoken of him as one who by
a happy stroke in fiction made his mark and fortune, and
finding his sentiment and self-interest agreeable to a
continued championship of collectivist doctrines, easily
and almost unconsciously drifted into taking the role of
prophet. Assuredly, they do not know their man. His
sincerity, his passion for truth, his faith in the near fulfillment of his dreams, were among his most striking
characteristics. His delicacy of health and his retiring
disposition made it impossible for him to assume the
work of a Marx, a Lassalle, an Owen or a Phillips; but
every task looking toward a wider diffusion of his principles which was consonant with his temperament and
his circumstances, he undertook gladly, energetically and
with an entire absence of self-interest.

Among reformers, who are prone, more than other
persons, to grade men's greatness by making identity of
theory with their own the prime test, there must be a
wide divergence in their estimates of Bellamy. His
work was too partisan, as between one school and another, to gain much credit from the adherents of other
schools. His Nationalism is State Socialism (using that
term in its broad and democratic meaning, as against the
perverted sense in which it is frequently used); to him

21

intellectual and moral freedom would be the necessary sequence of the exactest economic regulation through the medium of the State; and theories based upon this or that single economic factor, or those looking toward the establishment of communities loosely regulated, appealed to him as insufficient, or chaotic and unreformative. Naturally the advocates of such theories hold that Bellamy has not analyzed the present or correctly outlined the future society.

State Socialists ourselves, we unhesitatingly place his contribution to the world's progressive thought among the highest. The vision was true, and the effect upon his generation marvelous. He did not originate—even his insistence upon national as against international social evolution is a heritage from Goethe; he combined. He was a social architect, draining the world's models for his own. Marx, an economist microscopically examining details, studious of bases and strata, made ready the foundations; men like Lassalle were the energetic spirits who prompted us to the great task, and Bellamy was the draughtsman of the new social edifice. His art, his imagination, his logical sense of order, made his work great and abiding.

# Why a New Nation?

## By Edward Bellamy
### (*From The New Nation, January, 1894*)

W HY a New Nation? Why will not the old one do?

These are some of the reasons why it will not do: In the old nation, the system by which the work of life is carried on is a sort of perpetual warfare, a struggle, literally to the death, between men and men. It is a system by which the contestants are forced to waste in fighting more effort than they have left for work. The sordid and bitter nature of the struggle so hardens, for the most part, the relations of men to their fellows that in the domestic circle alone do they find exercise for the better, tenderer and more generous elements of their nature.

Another reason why the old nation will not do, is, that in it the people are divided, against nature, into classes: one very small class being the wealthy; another and much larger class being composed of those who maintain with difficulty a condition of tolerable comfort constantly shadowed by apprehension of its loss; with, finally, a vastly greater and quite preponderating class of very poor, who have no dependence even for a bare existence save a wage which is uncertain from day to day.

In the old nation, moreover, half the people—the women, are dependent upon the other half, the men, for the means of support; no other alternative being left them but to seek a beggarly pittance as workers in a labor market already overcrowded by men. In this old nation, the women are, indeed, as a sex, far worse off than the men; for, while the rich man is at least independent, the rich woman, while more luxuriously cared for, is as dependent for support on her husband's favor as the wife of the poorest laborer. Meanwhile, a great many women openly, and no one can tell how many secretly, unable to find men who will support them on more honorable terms, are compelled to secure their livelihood by the sale of their bodies, while a multitude of others are constrained to accept loveless marriage bonds.

In this old nation, a million strong men are even now vainly crying out for work to do, though the world needs so much more work done. Meanwhile, though the fathers and husbands can find no work, there is plenty always for the little children, who flock, in piteous armies, through the chilling mists of winter dawns into the factories.

In this old nation, not only does wealth devour poverty, but wealth devours wealth, and, year by year, the assets of the nation pass more swiftly and completely into the hands of a few score individuals out of 65,000,000 people.

In this old nation, year by year, the natural wealth of the land, the heritage of the people, is being wasted by the recklessness of individual greed. The forests are ravaged, the fisheries of river and sea destroyed, the fertility of the soil exhausted.

In this old nation, under a vain form of free political institutions, the inequalities of wealth and the irresistible influence of money upon a people devoured by want, are making nominally republican institutions a machine more convenient even than despotism for the purposes of plutocracy and plunder.

These are a few of the reasons why the old nation will not do, and these, in turn, are a few of the reasons why men are looking and longing for The New Nation:

In The New Nation, work will not be warfare, but fraternal co-operation toward a store in which all will share alike. Human effort, no longer wasted by battle and cross-purposes, will create an abundance previously impossible.

More important far, the conditions of labor under the plan of fraternal co-operation will tend as strongly to stimulate fraternal sentiments and affectionate relations among the workers as the present conditions tend to repress them. The kindly side of men will no longer be known only to their wives and children.

In The New Nation, there will be neither rich nor poor; all will be equal partners in the product of the national industrial organization.

In The New Nation, the dependence of one sex upon another for livelihood, which now poisons love and gives lust its opportunity, will be forever at an end. As equal and independent partners in the product of the nation, women will have attained an economical enfranchisement, without which no political device could help them. Prostitution will be a forgotten horror.

In The New Nation, there will be no unemployed. All will be enabled and required to do their part according to their gifts, save only those whom age, sickness or infirmity has exempted; and these, no longer as now trodden under foot, will be served and guarded as tenderly as are the wounded in battle by their comrades.

In The New Nation, the children will be cherished as precious jewels, inestimable pledges of the divine love to men. Though mother and father forsake them, the nation will take them up.

In The New Nation, education will be equal and universal, and will cover the entire period of life during which it is now enjoyed by the most favored classes.

In The New Nation, the wasting of the people's heritage will cease, the forests will be replanted, the rivers and seas repopulated, and fertility restored to exhausted lands. The natural resources of the country will be cared for and preserved as a common estate, and one to which the living have title only as trustees for the unborn.

In The New Nation, the debauching influence of wealth being banished, and the people raised to a real equality by equal education and resources, a true democratic and popular government will become possible as it never was before. For the first time in history the world will behold a true republic, rounded, full-orbed, complete—a republic, social, industrial, political.

26

# Why the Name Nationalism?

## By Sylvester Baxter

*(From The Nationalist, July, 1890)*

EDWARD EVERETT HALE, whole lifelong devotion to causes which the Nationalist movement now concretes, makes him indeed, one of its most honored and eminent pioneers, has recently found some fault with the name, as not sufficiently indicative of the principles involved.

Let us then consider the word inscribed upon our standard, and endeavor to show our good friend and great follower, Dr. Hale, and perhaps other good friends who may not have pondered the matter as long as we, that our word is the aptest we could have chosen. In the first place, we wanted a name that would appeal to all, because our movement, unlike socialism as commonly understood, is not a class movement, but for the whole country. After reforming here we shall be stronger to reform the world. This practical idea was clearly in Bellamy's mind when he wrote our great book. He says there: "It was not till a rearrangement of the industrial and social system on a higher ethical basis, and for the more efficient production of wealth, was recognized as the interest, not of one class, but equally of all classes, of rich and poor, cultured and ignorant, old and young, weak and strong, men and women, that there was any prospect that it would be achieved. Then the National party arose to carry it out by political methods. It probably took that name because it was to nationalize the functions of production and distribution. Indeed, it could not well have had any other name, for its purpose was to realize the idea of the nation with a grandeur and completeness never before conceived, not as an association of men for certain merely political functions affecting their happiness only remotely and superficially, but as a family, a vital union, a common life, a mighty heaven-touching tree whose leaves are its people, fed from its veins, and feeding it in turn. The most patriotic of all possible parties, it sought to justify patriotism and raise it from an instinct to a rational devotion, by making the native land, truly a fatherland, a father who kept the people alive and was not merely an idol for whom they were expected to die."

Does not this definition by Mr. Bellamy justify most nobly the name as the most appropriate that could have been chosen? The designations of the two prominent existing parties, Republican and Democratic, are neither of them distinctly characteristic; either might with equal appropriateness be borne by one party or the other. A name should inherently convey the character of the thing or principle behind it. Other names, suggested by our principles, are defective in this regard. "Collectivism," for instance, is too abstract, and lacks inspiring associations. "Socialism," on the other hand, whether justly or unjustly, is too suggestive in its associations; and to assume the dead-weight of the numerous prejudices which the word conveys in the mind of the general public—partly through the injudicious and often violent course of its followers, and partly through the lack of definiteness and consequent indiscriminate application to diverse and conflicting purposes—might handicap us heavily in the endeavor to rehabilitate and popularize it. The name conveys the impression, also, of limitations to "social" conditions, rather than applications to national and industrial or economic affairs; and it arouses mistrust and opposition through inference of intention to interfere with the more intimate concerns of society, such as family relations and the like. Moreover, and most important, socialism, as defined by its ablest exponents in this country, still clings to compromises with the old order, and would retain distinctions and gradations which must be abolished, else the evils now dominant would inevitably spring up again with all their baneful effects.

Nationalism, however, has no such drawback. More radical than socialism in its ideas, it differentiates itself further by being more conservative in its methods of applying them. Then, too, the associations of the word, Nationalism, are as lofty and inspiring as they are vital and definite. It would be hardy possible to stigmatize popularly a term so eminent; and a movement that gives an honor, a service and a comprehensiveness to national functions, will exalt nationality as never before in the public mind. Even in the infancy of our movement this is already perceptible by the way in which the name has taken popular hold.

There is, however, a seeming logical objection in the subordinate application of our principles to municipal conditions, such as in the local public control and ownership of functions and services like water-works, illuminating and heating supplies, etc. But it should be remembered that these are important steps toward the nationalization of industry; for with the complete realization of our system, the only essential political entities, besides the inclusive nation, would be the municipalities, to which the exercise of local functions would of course be delegated; just as functions of self-help are now par tially delegated to them by the various federative commonwealths, whose lines in turn are being gradually and surely effaced by the closer relation of the mass to the nation.

# Declaration of Principles

*(Edward Bellamy in The Nationalist, May 1889)*

THE principle of the Brotherhood of Humanity is one of the eternal truths that govern the world's progress on lines which distinguish human nature from brute nature.

The principle of competition is simply the application of the brutal law of the survival of the strongest and most cunning.

Therefore, so long as competition continues to be the ruling factor in our industrial system, the highest development of the individual cannot be reached, the loftiest aims of humanity cannot be realized.

No truth can avail unless practically applied. Therefore those who seek the welfare of man must endeavor to suppress the system founded on the brute principle of competition and put in its place another based on the nobler principle of association.

But in striving to apply this nobler and wiser principle to the complex conditions of modern life, we advocate no sudden or ill considered changes; we make no war upon individuals; we do not censure those who have accumulated immense fortunes simply by carrying to a logical end the false principle on which business is now based.

The combinations, trusts and syndicates of which the people at present complain, demonstrate the practicability of our basic principle of association. We merely seek to push this principle a little further and have all industries operated in the interest of all by the nation—the people organized—the organic unity of the whole people.

The present industrial system proves itself wrong by the immense wrongs it produces; it proves itself absurd by the immense waste of energy and material which is admitted to be its concomitant. Against this system we raise our protest; for the abolition of the slavery it has wrought and would perpetuate, we pledge our best efforts.

# Plutocracy or Nationalism—Which?

*(Address of Edward Bellamy at Tremont Temple, Boston, May 31, 1889\*)*

W HEN Rome was the world's center, it used to be said that all roads led to Rome; so now, when the burden upon the heart of the world is the necessity of evolving a better society, it may be said that all lines of thought lead to the social question. For the sake of clearness, however, I shall this afternoon take up but a single thread of a single line of argument, namely, the economic. I shall speak of the present tendency to the concentration of the industrial and commercial business of the country in few and constantly fewer hands. The "Trust," or "Syndicate," in which this tendency finds its fullest expression, is recognized as one of the most significant phenomena of the day. In seeking a comparison for the bewildering effect produced by the appearance of the Trust above the business horizon, one can only think of the famous comets of past centuries and the terrors their rays diffused, turning nations into flocks of sheep and perplexing kings with fear of change. The advent of the Trust marks a crisis more important than a hundred presidential elections rolled into one—no less a crisis, in fact, than the beginning of the end of the competitive system in industry. And the end is going to be rather near the beginning. It is in vain that the newspapers sit up nights with the patient and the legislatures feed

---

\*Reprinted by special permission from Marion Bellamy Earnshaw.

it with tonics.  It is moribund.  The few economists who still seriously defend the competitive system are heroically sacrificing their reputations in the effort to mask the evacuation of a position which, as nobody knows better than our hard-headed captains of industry, has become untenable.  Surely there have been few, if any, events in history on which the human race can be so unreservedly congratulated as the approaching doom of the competitive system.  From the beginning, Christianity has been at odds with its fundamental principle—the principle that the only title to the means of livelihood is the strength and cunning to get and keep. Between Christianity and the competitive system a sort of *modus vivendi* has indeed been patched up, but Christianity has not thriven upon it, and the friends of Christianity are today vigorously repudiating it.  As for the humane and philanthropic spirit, it has always found itself set at naught, and practically dammed up, by a system of which sordid self-seeking is so absolutely the sole idea that kindliness, humanity and generous feeling simply will not mix with it, while charity deranges the whole machine.

The final plea for any form of brutality in these days is that it tends to the survival of the fittest; and very properly this plea has been advanced in favor of the system which is the sum of all brutalities.  But the retort is prompt and final.  If this were indeed so, if the richest were the best, there would never have been any social question.  Disparities of condition would have been willingly endured, which were recognized as corresponding to virtue or public service.  But so far is this from being the case that the competitive system seems

34

rather to tend to the survival of the unfittest. Not that the rich are worse than the poor, but that the competitive system tends to develop what is worst in the character of all, whether rich or poor. The qualities which it discourages are the noblest and most generous that men have, and the qualities which it rewards are those selfish and sordid instincts which humanity can only hope to rise above by outgrowing. But perhaps the explanation of the panic which the critical condition of the competitive system excites in some quarters lies in a belief that whatever may be said as to the immoral aspects of it, it is nevertheless so potent a machine for the production of wealth as to be indispensable. If such a belief be entertained, it is certainly the most groundless of superstitions. The problem before any system of national industry is to get the greatest result out of the natural resources of a country and the capital and labor of a people. In what way then, let us inquire, has the competitive system undertaken to solve this problem? It would seem a matter of obvious common sense that it should of course proceed upon some carefully digested and elaborated system of work to begin with. We should expect to see a close and constant oversight to secure perfect cooperation and coordination between all departments of work and all the workers. But in fact the competitive system offers nothing of the sort. Instead of a carefully digested plan of operation, there is no general plan at all; there are as many plans as there are workers, some twenty millions. There is no general oversight even of an advisory sort. Every worker not only has his own plan but is his own commander-in-chief.

# EDWARD BELLAMY SPEAKS AGAIN!

Not only is there no cooperation between the workers, but each is doing all he possibly can to hinder those who are working near him. Finally, not only are they not working in cooperation, but they are not even working for the same end—that is, the general wealth; but each to get the most for himself. And this he does, as frequently as not, by courses not only not contributory to the general wealth, but destructive of it.

If one of you should apply the same method of planlessness, lack of oversight and utter lack of cooperation, to your own factory or farm, your friends would have you in an asylum in twenty-four hours, and be called long suffering at that. Not a man in the country would undertake to cultivate a quarter of an acre, not a woman would undertake Spring cleaning, without more plan, more system for economy of effort, than goes to the correlated management of the industries of the United States.

If you would form a vivid conception of the economical absurdity of the competitive system in industry, consider merely the fact that its only method of improving the quality or reducing the price of goods is by overdoing their production. Cheapness, in other words, can only result under competition from duplication and waste of effort. But things which are produced with waste of effort are really dear, whatever they may be called. Therefore, goods produced under competition are made cheap only by being made dear. Such is the *reductio ad absurdum* of the system. It is in fact often true that the goods we pay the least for are in the end the most expensive to the nation owing to the wasteful competition

36

which keeps down the price. All waste must in the end mean loss and, therefore, about once in seven years the country has to go into insolvency as the result of a system which sets three men to fighting for work which one man could do.

To speak of the moral iniquities of competition would be to enter on too large a theme for this time, and I only advert in passing to one feature of our present industrial system in which it would be hard to say whether inhumanity or economic folly predominated, and refer to the grotesque manner in which the burden of work is distributed. The industrial press-gang robs the cradle and the grave, takes the wife and mother from the fireside, and old age from the chimney-corner, while at the same time hundreds of thousands of strong men fill the land with clamors for an opportunity to work. The women and children are delivered to the task-masters, while the men can find nothing to do. There is no work for the fathers but there is plenty for the babies.

What then is the secret of this alarm over the approaching doom of a system under which nothing can be done properly without doing it twice, which can do no business without overdoing it, which can produce nothing without over-production, which in a land full of want cannot find employment for strong and eager hands, and finally which gets along at all only at the cost of a total collapse every few years, followed by a lingering convalescence?

When a bad king is mourned by his people, the conclusion must be that the heir to the throne is a worse case still. That appears to be, in fact, the explanation of the present distress over the decay of the competitive system. It is because there is fear of going from bad to worse, and that the little finger of combination will be thicker than the loins of competition; that while the latter system has chastised the people with whips, the Trust will scourge them with scorpions. Like the children of Israel in the desert, this new and strange peril causes the timid to sigh even for the iron rule of Pharaoh. Let us see if there be not also in this case a promised land, by the prospect of which faint hearts may be encouraged.

Let us first enquire whether a return to the old order of things, the free competitive system, is possible. A brief consideration of the causes which have led to the present world-wide movement for the substitution of combination in business for competition will surely convince any one that, of all revolutions, this is the least likely to go backward. It is a result of the increase in the efficiency of capital in great masses, consequent upon the inventions of the last and present generations. In former epochs the size and scope of business enterprises were subject to natural restrictions. There were limits to the amount of capital that could be used to advantage by one management. Today there are no limits, save the earth's confines, to the scope of any business undertaking; and not only no limit to the amount of capital that can be used by one concern, but an increase in the efficiency and security of the business proportionate to the amount of capital in it. The economies in management resulting from consolidation, as well as the control over the market resulting from the monopoly of a staple, are also solid business reasons for the advent of the

Trust.  It must not be supposed, however, that the principle of combination has been extended to those businesses only which call themselves Trusts.  That would be
greatly to under-estimate the movement.  There are
many forms of combination less close than the Trust, and
comparatively few businesses are now conducted without
some understanding approaching to a combination with
its former competitors—a combination tending constantly to become closer.

From the time that these new conditions began to prevail, the small businesses have been disappearing before
the larger; the process has not been so rapid as people
fancy whose attention has but lately been called to it.
For twenty years past the great corporations have been
carrying on a war of extermination against the swarm
of small industrial enterprises which are the red blood
corpuscles of a free competitive system and with the
decay of which it dies.  While the economists have been
wisely debating whether we could dispense with the principle of individual initiative in business, that principle
has passed away, and now belongs to history.  Except
in a few obscure corners of the business world, there is
at present no opportunity for individual initiative in business unless backed by a large capital; and the size of the
capital needed is rapidly increasing.  Meanwhile, the
same increase in the efficiency of capital in masses, which
has destroyed the small businesses, has reduced the giants
which have destroyed them to the necessity of making
terms with one another.  As in Bulwer Lytton's fancy
of the coming race, the people of the Vril-ya had to give
up war because their arms became so destructive as to

threaten mutual annihilation, so the modern business world finds that the increase in the size and powers of the organizations of capital demands the suppression of competition between them, for the sake of self-preservation.

The first great group of business enterprises which adopted the principle of combining, instead of competing, made it necessary for every other group sooner or later to do the same or perish. For as the corporation is more powerful than the individual, so the syndicate overtops the corporation. The action of governments to check this logical necessity of economical evolution can produce nothing more than eddies in a current which nothing can check. Every week sees some new tract of what was once the great open sea of competition, wherein merchant adventurers used to fare forth with little capital besides their courage and come home loaded—every week now sees some new tract of this once open sea inclosed, dammed up, and turned into the private fish-pond of a syndicate.

I would also incidentally call your attention to the fact that these syndicates are largely foreign. Our new industrial lords are largely to be absentees. The British are invading the United States in these days with a success brilliantly in contrast with their former failures in that line. It is no wonder in these days, when the political basis of aristocracy is going to pieces, that foreign capitalists should rush into a market where industrial dukedoms, marquisates and baronies, richer than ever a king distributed to his favorites, are for sale. To say that from the present look of things the substantial consolidation of the various groups of industries in the country, under a few score great syndicates, is likely to be complete within fifteen years, is certainly not to venture a wholly rash statement.

So great an economic change as is involved in taking the conduct of the country's industries out of the hands of the people, and concentrating them in the management of a few great Trusts, could not, of course, be without important social reaction; and this is a reaction which is going to affect peculiarly what is called, in the hateful jargon of classes which we hope some day to do away with, the middle class. It is no longer a question merely for the poor and uneducated what they are to do with their work; but for the educated and well-to-do, also, where they are to find business to do and business investments to make. This difficulty cannot fail constantly to increase, as one tract after another of the formerly free field of competition is inclosed by a new syndicate. The middle class, the business class, is being turned into a proletarian class.

It is not difficult to forecast the ultimate issue of the concentration of industry if carried out on the lines at present indicated. Eventually, and at no very remote period, society must be divided into a few hundred families of prodigious wealth on the one hand, a professional class dependent upon their favor but excluded from equality with them and reduced to the state of lackeys; and underneath a vast population of working men and women, absolutely without hope of bettering a condition which would year by year sink them more and more hopelessly into serfdom.

# EDWARD BELLAMY SPEAKS AGAIN!

This is not a pleasant picture, but I am sure it is not an exaggerated statement of the social consequences of the syndicate system carried out according to the plans of its managers. Are we going to permit the American people to be rounded up, corralled and branded as the dependents of some hundreds of great American and English families? It is well never to despair of the Republic, but it is well to remember that republics are saved not by a vague confidence in their good luck, but by the clear vision and courageous action of their citizens.

What, then, is the outcome? What way lies the Promised Land which we may reach? For back to Egypt we cannot go. The return to the old system of free competition and the day of small things is not a possibility. It would involve a turning backward of the entire stream of modern material progress.

If the nation does not wish to turn over its industries —and that means its liberties as well—to an industrial oligarchy, there is but one alternative; it must assume them itself. Plutocracy or Nationalism is the choice which, within ten years, the people of the United States will have virtually made.

Pray observe, ladies and gentlemen, that your argument is not with me, or with those of us who call ourselves Nationalists. We are not forcing upon you this alternative. The facts of the present state and tendencies of national affairs are doing it. Your controversy is with them, not with us. Convince yourself and your friends that this talk about the invasion and appropriation of the field of general business by Trusts and Syndicates is all nonsense; satisfy yourself from a careful

# PLUTOCRACY OR NATIONALISM—WHICH?

study of the news of the day that there is really no tendency toward the concentration in the hands of a comparatively few powerful organizations of the means of the nation's livelihood, and you can afford to disregard us entirely. Nothing is more certain than that we cannot make a revolution with mere words, or unless the facts are with us. Once admit, however, that the Trusts and Syndicates are facts, and that business is rapidly being concentrated in their hands, and if you do not propose to submit to the state of things which these admitted facts portend, you have no choice but to be Nationalists. The burning issue of the period now upon us is to be, is already, Nationalism against Plutocracy. In its fierce heat the ties of old party allegiances are destined ere long to dissolve like wax.

There have been many movements for a nobler order of society which should embody and illustrate brotherly love, but they have failed because the time was not right; that is to say, because the material tendencies of the age did not work with the moral. Today they work together. Today it matters little how weak the voice of the preacher may be, for the current of affairs, the logic of events, is doing his work and preaching his sermon for him. This is why there is ground today for a higher-hearted hope that a great deliverance for humanity is at hand than was ever before justified. When sun and moon together pull the sea, a mighty tide is sure to come. So today, when the spiritual and economic tendencies of the time are for once working together; when the spirit of this age, and the divine spirit of all ages, for once are on the same side, hope becomes reason, and confidence is but common sense. Many, perhaps, have a vague idea of what Nationalism is, and may wish to know in just what ways our national assumption of the industries of the country is going to affect the people beneficially. Briefly it may be said that the result of this action will be to make the nation an equal industrial partnership of its members as it already is an equal political partnership. The people will have formed themselves into a great joint stock company for the general business of maintaining and enjoying life. In this company every man and woman will be an equal stockholder, and the annual dividends will constitute their means of subsistence. While all share alike in the profits of the business, all will share according to their strength in its service, the nation undertaking to provide employment for all adapted to their gifts and guaranteeing the industrious against the idle by making industrial service obligatory. In effect the nation will then have become a universal insurance company for the purpose of assuring all its members against want, oppression, accident, or disability of whatever sort. It will be a mighty trust holding all the assets of society, moral, intellectual, and material, not only for the use of the present and passing generation, but for the benefit of the future race, looking to the ends of the world and the judgment of God. This is Nationalism.

Economically, it will be observed that the Nationalization of industry presents the logical, conclusive, and complete form of the evolution from competition toward combination which is now in progress. Every economical argument for the partial consolidation of industry already being effected, together with many new ones, tends to prove that a complete National consolidation would create a system better adapted to wealth production than any the world has seen.

It is important to state that while the economic movement toward consolidation is greatly hastening the nationalization of industries, that result will belong strictly to another line of evolution—the political. That is to say, the National idea—which is that of the union of a people to use the collective strength for the common protection and welfare,—distinctly and logically involved from the beginning the eventual nationalization of industry and the placing of the livelihood of the people under the national guarantee. If this be the true conception of a nation, then how preposterous is the notion that the mere exclusive possession, as against foreign nations, of a tract of land, in any true sense constitutes nationality. The house-lot is not a house. Such a community has merely secured a place on which to build a nation, that is all. The nation may be built or not. If it is built, it will consist in a social structure so roofed over and meetly joined together and so arranged within in all its details, as to provide in the highest possible degree for the happiness and welfare of all its people. Where are any such nations? you may well ask. And I reply that there are none, and never have been any. We consider that the time is now arrived for building such nations, and that the first such nation will be built in America. We call ourselves Nationalists because we have faith in this true nation that is to be, and have given our hearts and our allegiance to it while yet it is unborn.

The fact that the use of the collective power for the

45

common benefit was first made in protecting the people in war, arose from the fact that the first necessity of every community, the condition of its further development, was protection from external foes. On the other hand, let it be observed that the only object of this protection from external interference was to provide the opportunity for internal development—that is, for building the social structure. It is thus self-evident that no nation has an excuse for existing at all in which this process of internal social evolution is not going on. The shell of the egg is necessary to protect the vital principle within, during the process of evolving to a complete life. That is its only use. A nation which, having perfected its external organization, stops short there, has failed of the object of its existence, and can be compared to nothing more savory than an addled egg.

Consider the consequences which have followed the arrest of the development of the national idea at the point of division between the foreign relations of the people and their internal affairs. In war, the nation is the champion and the vindicator, against the world, of the rights of person and property of its humblest citizen. But let peace come, and this great archangel shrinks to the stature and functions of a policeman. Do you protest in indignation against such an incongruity, do you demonstrate that in one week, the sufferings of citizens from the oppressions, cruelties and maladjustments of industry exceed in quantity and poignancy all that the nation has ever suffered from foreign foes in its whole history? You will be told in reply that this is all quite as it should be. It will be explained to you that the nation has no business at all to concern itself for the welfare of its people, except as and when that welfare may be threatened by foreigners. It has no business to take cognizance of any trouble its people may be in, much less to take steps to remedy it, unless it can be shown to be the result in some way of foreign aggression. If a citizen desires the nation to take an interest in his welfare, it is of no use at all for him to stay at home and suffer. The nation will not regard such sufferings. It is far-sighted and can only see the afflictions of its people when they are a great way off. If the citizen would know how dear he is to the nation, let him go to the ends of the earth and get some foreigner to abuse him. Then indeed will he be astonished to find how devoted to his rights and his welfare his countrymen are. The very nation, which, so long as he stayed at home, did not care a pin whether he starved or lived, will incontinently, and without even stopping to find out whether he is in the right or not, enthusiastically sacrifice a hundred thousand soldiers, and double the national debt in his behalf.

May it not be well asked if mankind is, in any other respect, the victim of a theory at once so preposterous and so tragical in its consequences as that which limits the nation's guardianship of its people to their protection from foreigners? Is it any wonder that there should have arisen a sect of social reformers, under the name of Internationalists, who protest that the national organizations do but cumber the ground and block the progress of humanity? What is the use, may indeed be asked, of national distinctions, if they only fence off different sets of people to be fleeced and exploited separately? As well make the world all one pen, and save the expense of forts, fleets and armies. Nationalists, on the other hand, while admitting that the nations stand utterly condemned by their failure in the premises, yet maintain that through and by the nations, when they shall be aroused to assume and discharge their full responsibility for their people, is to come the deliverance of man.

We seek the final answer to the social question not in revolution, but in evolution; not in destruction, but in fulfillment,—the fulfillment of the hitherto stunted development of the nation according to its logical intent.

We hear much of the duty of the citizen to the country. We cannot hear too much of that, but it is time something were also said of the duty of the country to the citizen. We are taught, and taught rightly, that it is the duty of the people to die for the nation in war. Is it not time we heard something of the duty of the nation to keep the people from starving in peace? Are not these obligations properly to be regarded as reciprocal? Truly it appears to me that the account between this nation and its people shows the nation most grievously in debt to the people.

Yesterday was celebrated the sacred civic festival of our American year. As we laid the garlands upon the graves of our heroes, the memory of the day came freshly to our minds when they went forth to battle at the call of the country. We saw them turn away from wife and sweetheart, and from the dear kisses of their little ones—from the embraces of those who would die for them—to die for the country; gladly giving their heart's

48

blood to cement her walls; eagerly proffering their tender bodies for her living barricades. How then has the country deserved, and how does she repay, this incredible devotion? this worship which the gods might envy? this tenderness which is not given to women?

Surely we may reasonably expect to find that the country cares well for such devoted citizens, and for their women and children, and that, in all ways which the collective might can support, protect and sustain them, it is employed to those ends. No doubt she sees to it that the workers who feed the world are not rewarded with oppression, but are at least guaranteed absolute security in their portion of the livelihood they create for all. To the sick, weak and infirm, and those who have no helper, we shall surely find the nation to be as the shadow of a great rock in a weary land. To the women, the nation is doubtless careful to lend of its mighty strength, that thereby they may be borne up, and not fall beneath the feet of their strong brothers; while as for the children—surely for them the nation reserves its peculiar tenderness and most vigilant watch-care. In these ways at least, as well as in a thousand others, we may confidently expect to find the nation using its strength to safeguard the people who in time of need so heroically succored it.

But no; not the least of these functions of justice, oversight, sustenance, and protection, do we find even an attempt to execute. The nation sits on high, indifferently looking on, while the people rend one another in a brutal and merciless struggle for existence, in which the weak, the old, the sick are trampled under foot. Serenely the nation looks on, while little children are driven to toil; while armies of women sell themselves for bread; while the sick and the old suffer want till the clods of the valley seem sweet to them and the earth is sodden with the tears of the widow and fatherless; while education becomes the privilege of the rich, work of the fortunate, and ignorance and poverty brood over the face of the land like a dense cloud, forbidding the light of the sun and the consolation of the stars to those who toil beneath.

Why then, since this is so, do not the people revile the country when she cries for help? How shall their passionate loyalty to a nation so ungrateful be accounted for? Were those heroes whose graves we decorated yesterday, victims of some strange madness such as has led men before in frenzy to sacrifice themselves to senseless idols? Not so. We are here come, rather, to a sacred mystery. The instinct of patriotism, like the instinct of maternity, is prophetic, and looks to the future, not the present, for its full vindication. The impulse that prompts the mother to sacrifice her life for the child, as yet not even able to understand her love, is implanted to the end that men worthy of sacrifice and capable of gratitude may later stand on the earth. So the instinct of patriotism—with difficulty to be reconciled with reason, while yet the nation so utterly fails to discharge a nation's responsibilities,—will be abundantly justified when the nation shall at last awake to them. In that day it will appear that the heroes who died that the nation might live did even better than they knew. In that day their sacrifice will be justified, and extolled in the eyes of all;

their graves will blossom anew with the redoubled gratitude of men, and the spirits of the patriotic dead of all
generations will see of the travail of their souls and be
satisfied.

# Nationalism—Principles, Purposes

*(Address of Edward Bellamy at Tremont Temple, Boston, on the Nationalist Club Anniversary, Dec. 19, 1889)*

N O FACT is better established by experience or more easily demonstrable by reason than that no republic can long exist unless a substantial equality in the wealth of citizens prevails. Wealth is power in its most concentrated, most efficient and most universally applicable form. In the presence of great disparities of wealth, social equality is at an end, industrial independence is destroyed, while mere constitutional stipulations as to the equal rights of citizens politically or before the law, become ridiculous.

One hundred years ago this Republic was founded upon a substantial equality in the condition of the people. It was not an equality established by law, but a condition resulting from a general state of poverty. For the first fifty years the increase in the wealth of the country was gradual, but within the last thirty years, owing to great mechanical and commercial inventions, it has multiplied by leaps and bounds, no longer growing from decade to decade by arithmetical, but by geometrical ratio. Instead of chiefly tending to enhance the general welfare of the people, this wealth has been mainly appropriated by a small class. At the present time the property of 100,000 men in the United States aggregates more than the total possessions of the rest of the people. Ten thousand people own nearly the whole of New York City with its 2,000,000 population. The entire bonded debt of the United States is held by 71,000 persons only, and over 60 per cent of it is in the hands of 23,000 persons. A volume of similar details might be furnished, but the situation may be summed up in one of the characteristic phrases of modern business, as follows: Mainly within thirty years 100,000 Americans have succeeded in "freezing out" their 65,000,000 co-partners as to more than half the assets of the concern, and at the rate of the last thirty years, within thirty years more will have secured the remainder.

That is the situation which has created the need for Nationalism. Those are the facts which account for the rapidity of its spread among the people.

For the sake of clearness let us distinguish the evil effects of the concentration of wealth in the hands of a few, as political, social and industrial. First as to the political effects.

The great corporations and combinations of capital dwarf our municipalities, overtop our States and are able to dictate to our National Legislature. The extent to which intimidation and bribery are employed to influence popular elections taints with the suspicion of fraud nearly all verdicts of the ballot when the majority is not large. Even in the grand appeal to the Nation the money power, by judicious concentration of corruption funds upon close States, is able to set at naught the will of the people. The titles of the Presidents of the Republic are no longer clear. What money cannot effect at the polls, by intimidation or by bribery, it does not hesitate to attempt by the corruption of individual legislators. Our municipal Council chambers are too often mere auction rooms, where public franchises are sold to the highest briber.· The Legislatures of some of our greatest States are commonly said to be owned by particular corporations. The United States Senate is known as a "rich men's club," and in the lower House of Congress the schemes of capital have only to meet the sham opposition of the demagogue.

Socially, the vast disparities of wealth afford on every side inhuman contrasts of cruel want and inordinate luxury. The dazzling illustrations of pomp and power, which are the prizes of wealth, have lent to the pursuit of gain, at all times sufficiently keen, a feverish intensity and desperation never seen before in this or any other country. The moderate rewards of persistent industry seem contemptible in the midst of a universal speculative fever. In all directions the old ways of legitimate business and steady application are being abandoned for speculative projects, gambling operations and all manner of brigandage under forms of law. The spectacle presented in many instances of great riches, notoriously won by corrupt methods, has undermined the foundations of honesty. The epidemic of fraud and embezzlement, which today renders wealth so insecure, results from the general recognition that the possession of property, though it may have a legal title, is very commonly without a moral one. This is the deplorable explanation of the cynical tolerance of fraud by public opinion. Property will not, in the long run, be respected which is without some reasonable basis in industry or desert, and it is justly believed that much of the wealth of today could not stand inquiry into the means of its getting.

The consequences of the appropriation of the Nation's wealth by a few, and its further concentration by means of corporations and syndicates, have made possible a policy of monopolizing the control and profits of the industries of the country never before even imagined as among the possible perils of society. Hitherto, when oligarchies have usurped the political control of nations, they have left the conduct of business to the vulgar, but our new order of "nobility" is laying its foundations deeper by obtaining absolute mastery of the means of support of the people.

The effect of the concentration and combination of capital in the conduct of business has been directly to bring the wage-earner more completely than ever under the thumb of the employer. A chief object of combination is to control prices by restricting production—that is to say, employment. While the competition among wage-earners for work is thus made more desperate, they are placed at the mercy of employers by the fact that in so far as employers are consolidated they no longer compete with one another.

But there could be no greater mistake than to fancy that the manual worker is peculiarly a victim of the present situation. The business men, the small tradesmen and manufacturers and the professional classes are suffering quite as much and have quite as much to dread from monopoly as has the poorest class of laborers.

As one after another the different departments of business, productive and distributive, pass under the

single or syndicate control of the great capitalists, the
so-called middle-class, the business men with moderate
capital and plenty of wit, who used to conduct the business of the country, are crowded out of their occupation
and rendered superfluous. No doubt the substitution of
single for multiple control and the suppression of middlemen represents an economy. But the economy does not
benefit the consumer, but goes to swell the profits of
the capitalists. Meanwhile, fathers who were set up by
their fathers in business find it impossible to do the like
for their sons. There is now almost no opportunity left
for starting in business in a moderate way; none, indeed,
unless backed by large capital. What this means is, that
we are rapidly approaching a time when there will be
no class between the very rich, living on their capital,
and a vast mass of wage and salary receivers absolutely
dependent upon the former class for their livelihood.
Meanwhile, as the immediate effect of the closing up of
business careers to young men, the professions are being
overcrowded to the starvation point. The problem before young men coming out of school or college, where
to find a place in the world, was never so hard as now.
Plutocracy is indeed fast leaving no place for a young
man of independent and patriotic spirit, save in the party
of Radical Social Reform.

The agricultural interests of the country are passing
under the yoke of the money power quite as rapidly as
the other forms of industry. The farmers are becoming
expropriated by the operation of something like a universal mortgage system, and unless this tendency shall
be checked the next generation of farmers will be a gen-

eration of tenants-at-will. The agrarian conditions of Ireland bid fair in no long time to be reproduced in portions of the West.

Such, fellow-countrymen, is the condition of political corruption, of social rottenness, of moral degeneracy, of industrial oppression, confusion and impending ruin which has resulted from the overthrow of our republican equality by the money power. If you would learn how republics perish, shut up your musty histories of Greece and Rome and look about you.

In time the money power is bound to seek protection from the rising discontent of the masses in a stronger form of government, and then the republic, long before dead, will be put out of sight. Then it will be too late to resist. Now it is not too late. The republic is being taken from us, but it is still possible to bring it back. Soon it will be too late to do so, but today there is yet time, though there is none to waste.

The Nationalists of the United States ask the cooperation of their fellow-countrymen to bring back the republic. To that end they propose a reorganization of the industrial system which shall restore the equality of the people and secure it by a perpetual guarantee.

In advocating a plan to secure equality we propose to graft no new or strange principle upon the republican idea, but the exercise of a power implied in the very idea of republicanism as ultimately necessary to its preservation. A republic is a form of government based upon and guaranteeing to all citizens a common interest in the national concern. That interest can be common only in proportion as it is substantially an equality of

interest. The time has now come in America as it has
come sooner or later in the history of all republics, when
by the increase of wealth and by gross disparity in its
distribution, this equality in its three aspects—political,
social, industrial—is threatened with complete subver-
sion. In order, under the changed conditions, to make
good the original pledge of the republic to its citizens, it
has become necessary to re-establish and maintain by
some deliberate plan that economic equality, the basis
of all other sorts of equality which, when the republic was
established, existed in a substantial degree by nature.
The question is not of assuming a new obligation, but
whether the original ends and purposes of the republican
compact shall be repudiated. We demand that the republic keep faith with the people, and propose a plan
of industrial reorganization which seems to us the only
possible means by which that faith can be kept. We
are the true conservative party, because we are devoted to
the maintenance of republican institutions against the
revolution now being effected by the money power. We
propose no revolution, but that the people shall resist a
revolution. We oppose those who are overthrowing the
republic. Let no mistake be made here. We are not
revolutionists, but counter-revolutionists.

But while the guarantee of the equality of citizens is
thus a measure amply justified and necessitated by merely patriotic and national considerations, without looking
further for arguments, we do, in proposing this action,
look both further and higher, to the ends of the earth,
indeed, and the ultimate destiny of the race.

While historic, political and economic conditions require that this movement should be conducted on national lines by each people for itself, we hold the economic equality of all men a principle of universal application, having for its goal the eventual establishment of a brotherhood of humanity as wide as the world and as numerous as mankind. Those who believe that all men are brothers, and should so regard one another, must believe in the equality of men, for equals only can be brothers. Even brothers by blood do but hate each other the more bitterly for the tie when the inheritance is unequally parted between them, while strangers are presently made to feel like brothers by equality of interest and community of loss and gain. Therefore we look to the establishment of equality among men as the physical basis necessary to realize that brotherhood of humanity regarded by the good and wise of all ages as the ideal state of society. We believe that a wonderful confluence, at the present epoch, of material and moral tendencies throughout the world, but especially in America, has made a great step in the evolution of humanity, not only possible, but necessary for the salvation of the race. We are surrounded by perils from which the only way of escape is the way upward.

The plan of industrial reorganization which Nationalism proposes is the very simple and obvious one of placing the industrial duty of citizens on the ground on which their military duty already rests. All able-bodied citizens are held bound to fight for the nation, and, on the other hand, the nation is bound to protect all citizens, whether they are able to fight or not. Why not extend this accepted principle to industry, and hold every able-

60

bodied citizen bound to work for the nation, whether with mind or muscle, and, on the other hand, hold the nation bound to guarantee the livelihood of every citizen, whether able to work or not. As in military matters the duty to fight is conditioned upon physical ability, while the right of protection is conditioned only upon citizenship, so would we condition the obligation to work upon the strength to work, but the right to support upon citizenship only.

The result would be to substitute for the present ceaseless industrial civil war, of which it would be hard to say whether it is more brutal or more wasteful, a partnership of all the people, a great joint stock company to carry on the business on the country for the benefit of all equally, women with men, sick with well, strong with weak. This plan of a national business partnership of equals we hold not only to be demonstrably practicable, but to constitute as truly the only scientific plan for utilizing the energy of the people in wealth production, as it is the only basis for society consistent with justice, with the sentiment of brotherhood, with the teachings of the founder of Christianity, and, indeed, of the founders of all the great religions.

The realization of the proposed plan of industry requires as the preliminary step the acquisition by the nation through its government, national and municipal, of the present industrial machinery of the country. It follows, therefore, that the Nationalists' programme must begin with the progressive nationalization of the industries of the United States. In proposing this course we are animated by no sentiment of bitterness toward individuals or classes. In antagonizing the money power we antagonize not men but a system. We advocate no rash or violent measures, or such as will produce derangement of business or undue hardship to individuals. We aim to change the law by the law, and the Constitution, if necessary, by constitutional methods. As to the order in which industries should be nationalized, priority should naturally be given to those the great wealth of which renders them perilous to legislative independence, to those which deal extortionately with the public or oppressively with employees, to those which are highly systematized and centralized and to those which can be readily assimilated by existing departments of government.

The following are some of the measures in the line of this policy for which the country appears to be quite ready:

First—The nationalization of the railroads whether by constituting the United States perpetual receiver of all lines, to manage the same for the public interest, paying over to the present security-holders, pending the complete establishment of nationalism, such reasonable dividends on a just valuation of the property as may be earned, or by some other practicable method not involving hardship to individuals.

The nationalization of the railroads is advisable for reasons apart from the Nationalist programme proper. Firstly, the railroad corporations, by the corrupt use of their vast wealth to procure and prevent legislation, are among the most formidable of the influences which are debauching our government. Secondly, the power they wield irresponsibly over the prosperity of cities, states and entire sections of the country, ought to be in the hands only of the general Government. Thirdly, the desperate rivalry of the railroads, with its incidents of reckless extension, duplication and rate wars, has long been a chief waste of the National resources and a cause of periodical business crises. Fourthly, the financial management of a large portion of the railroad system, together with its use for speculative purposes, has rendered railroad financiering the most gigantic gambling and general swindling business ever carried on in any country. Fifthly, the convenience and safety of the traveling public demand a uniform and harmonious railroad system throughout the country, nor is it likely that anything less will bring to an end the cruel slaughter of railroad employees now carried on by the corporations.

A second measure for which the people are certainly quite ready is the nationalization of the telegraphic and telephone services, and their addition to the Post Office, with which, as departments of transmission of intelligence, they should properly always have been connected.

Third—We propose that the express business of the country be assumed by the post-offices, according to the successful practices of other countries.

Fourth—We propose that the coal-mining business which at present is most rapaciously conducted as respects the public, and most oppressively as regards a great body of laborers, be nationalized, to the end that the mines may be continuously worked to their full capacity, coal furnished consumers at cost and the miners humanely dealt with. It is suggested that all mines here-

63

after discovered or opened shall be regarded as public property subject to just compensation for land.

Fifth—We propose that municipalities generally shall undertake lighting, heating, running of street-cars and such other municipal services as are now discharged by corporations, to the end that such services may be more cheaply and effectually rendered; that a fruitful source of political corruption be cut off and a large body of laborers be brought under humaner conditions of toil.

Pending the municipalization of all such services as have been referred to, Nationalists enter a general protest against the grant to corporations of any further franchises whether relating to transit, light, heat, water or other public services.

It is to be understood that all nationalized and municipalized businesses should be conducted at cost for use and not for profit, the amount at present paid in taxes by such businesses, being, however, charged upon them.

It is an essential feature of the method of Nationalism that as fast as industries are nationalized or municipalized, the conditions of the workers in them shall be placed upon a wholly humane basis. The hours of labor will be made reasonable, the compensation adequate, the conditions safe and healthful. Support in sickness, with pensions for disabled and superannuated workers, will be guaranteed.

The question will be asked, "How is this great force of public employees to be placed beyond the power of politicians and administrations to use for partisan purposes?" Nationalists respond by proposing a plan for organizing and maintaining all public departments of business that shall absolutely deprive parties or politicians of any direct or arbitrary power over their membership, either as to appointment, promotion or removal.

In the first place, it is understood that upon the nationalization of any business the existing force of employees and functionaries would be as a body retained. It is proposed that the service should be forthwith strictly graded and subsequently recruited exclusively by admissions to the lowest grade. All persons desiring to enter the service should be free to file applications at the proper bureau upon passing certain simple mental or physical tests, not competitive in character and adapted only to minimum grade of qualifications. Upon vacancies occurring in the force or a need of increase, the desired additions should be taken from the list of applicants on file, either in order of filed applications or, more perfectly to prevent fraud, by the drawing of the requisite number of names from a wheel containing the entire list of eligibles.

The chief of the department should be appointed at the discretion of the political executive, whether of city, state or nation, in order that responsibility for the general management of the business might be brought home to an elective officer. With this exception, and perhaps the further exceptions in some cases of the chiefs of a few important subordinate branches of the service, all positions should be filled by promotion in order of grades, such promotions to be determined by superiority of record and with certain requirements of length of service. While the chief should have power of suspension, no discharge from the service should take place save by verdict of a tribunal expressly erected for that purpose, before which all charges of fault or incompetence, whether by superior against subordinate, by subordinate against superior or by the outside public against members of the force, should be laid.

It is believed that such a plan of organization would absolutely prevent administrative coercion of members of the public service for partisan ends, and it is urgently recommended by Nationalists that it be immediately applied to the Post-Office and all other business departments of the general Government, to the employees and to the public works department of all municipalities.

The nationalization of the several great branches of public service and productions which have been enumerated would directly affect, greatly for the better, the condition of a million and a half of workers.

Here truly would be a bulwark against capitalism, against corporate usurpation, against industrial oppression. Here would be a mighty nucleus for the coming industrial army. Here, too, would be a great body of consumers whose needs would suggest and whose demands would sustain the beginning of the coming National distributive and productive system.

Even a single industry organized on such a basis as described and guaranteeing to its toilers security, health, safety, dignity and justice would be an object lesson of the advantage of Nationalism, even in its beginnings, which would greatly hasten the general adoption of the system. As a measure which cannot wait, seeing that at best, the consequences of its postponement must con-

66

tinue to be felt long after it is effected, we urge that such partisan support as may be needful to enable them to attend school to the age of seventeen at least, be provided under proper guards by the State for the children of parents unable to maintain them without aid from their labor, and that with this provision the employment of children should be unconditionally forbidden, and their education made rigidly compulsory, to the end that equality of educational opportunities for all be established.

Seeing that it would be manifestly inconsistent to make the education of our children compulsory while permitting the unlimited importation of adult ignorance and vice, a necessary complement to any system of education would be such regulation of foreign immigration as, without prejudice to honest intelligent poverty, should prevent the importation of persons grossly illiterate in their own language, of the defective and of criminals, merely political offenses not being considered crimes.

In reviewing the measures which have been mentioned as substantially representing, according to my belief, the present demands of Nationalists, it is observable that there is not one of them which is not demanded by considerations of humanity and public expediency quite without reference to Nationalism. A man has no need to be a Nationalist at all to advocate them. They have been freely and often favorably discussed by the press for years, and the leading political economists of this country and Europe are on record in favor of most if not all of them. As to some of the most important of these propositions, it is altogether probable that a majority of the American people, if they could be polled today would favor them. Nationalists may be, as some say, a very extravagant and fantastical set of people, but there is certainly nothing fantastical about the plan of action which they propose. There is not even anything which can be said to be greatly in advance of public opinion. This moderation is not accidental, nor yet a result of policy, but a necessary consequence of the method of Nationalism, which is essentially gradual and progressive rather than abrupt or violent, the method of evolution as opposed to that of revolution.

As to the relation of Nationalism to certain political and social issues of the day, a few words may be pertinent.

First, as to the tariff question. When the nation conducts all business for all, the common interest in every improvement will create a far stronger motive than now exists for all sorts of experiments and improvements in home industry, but owing to the public control of the production, tariffs will no longer be necessary as now to encourage private persons to undertake such new experiments. They will be tried as Government experiments are now tried, costing the country only the expense of the experimental stations, the Nation without prejudice to the experiment, continuing, if expedient, to buy in the cheapest market till its own is the cheapest.

The sectional jealousies based upon industrial rivalry, which now make States and cities enemies of each other's prosperity, and create sentiments of disunion will disappear when a National pooling of interests shall interest all equally in the prosperity of all.

# NATIONALISM—PRINCIPLES, PURPOSES

As to the race issue, the industrial discipline imposed by Nationalism, while of general benefit to the white population of the South in common with that of the North, will be an ideal system for developing, guiding and elevating the recently emancipated colored race. It should be distinctly stated that the National plan will put an end to every form of sexual slavery and place feminine freedom and dignity upon an unassailable basis by making women independent of men for the means of support. We consider that by no method less radical can women's rightful equality with men be established, or, if established, maintained.

The evils of intemperance have their strongest roots in the brutalizing conditions of existing society, in the poverty of the masses, their gross ignorance, their misery and despair, in the slavish dependence of women and children upon men, and in the interest of a large class of tradesmen in the sale of intoxicants. If this be true, then the abolition of poverty, the universality of the best education, the complete enfranchisement of women, with a system of distribution which will destroy all personal motive for stimulating the sale of intoxicants, constitute surely the most promising as well as the most radical line of true temperance reform.

While the nationalizing of land in such time and by such methods as shall involve least hardships to any is a part of the National plan, and while the Nationalists meanwhile favor all practicable measures to prevent land monopoly and protect tenants and farmers, they are not persuaded that any measure applying to land alone would

69

furnish a sufficient remedy for existing industrial and social troubles.

While sympathizing with all efforts of workers to obtain small immediate improvements in their condition, Nationalists would have them reflect that no great improvements can be gained, and if gained, can be secure, under the present industrial system, and that the only effectual and peaceable way of replacing that system by a better one is offered by Nationalism. It is also pointed out that the plan of Nationalism, by the humane and just conditions which will be secured to the employees of every industry, as it comes under the public control, offers not only the greatest ultimate results, but the speediest and surest way for immediately benefiting great bodies of workers absolutely without a risk of derangement to business.

One hundred years ago, after immemorial years of repression, the human passion for liberty, for equality, for brotherhood burst forth, convulsing Europe and establishing America. There is at hand another and far mightier outburst of the same forces, the results of which will be incomparably more profound, more far-reaching and more beneficent. Men now past middle age are likely to see in Europe the last throne fall, and in America the first complete and full-orbed republic arise, a republic at once political, industrial and social.

It is instructive for Americans to remember that there is scarcely any argument brought today against Nationalism which was not in substance brought against the experiment of political equality undertaken in this country a century ago; scarcely one which does not spring from the same low and suspicious estimate of human nature, the same distrust of the people, the same blind belief in personal and class leadership and authority; scarcely one which was not, as to principle, answered a hundred years ago by Madison, Hamilton and Jay in the 'Federalist'. And, indeed, how could it be otherwise? For what we propose is but the full development of the same republican experiment which the fathers undertook, a development now become necessary if we would preserve that experiment from ignominious failure.

In advocating equal rights for all as the only solution for the social and industrial problems of today, Nationalism follows the lines laid down by the founders of the Republic and proves itself the legitimate heir to the traditions and the spirit of 1776. Guided by those traditions, sustained by that spirit, we cannot fail.

# What Nationalism Means

## By Edward Bellamy

*(From The Contemporary Review, July, 1890\*)*

I N THE January number of this Review appeared an article by M. Emile de Laveleye, entitled "Two New Utopias." A project of industrial reform, recently outlined by M. Charles Secretan, figures as one of these Utopias, while the other is the plan of national cooperation described in "Looking Backward," and known in the United States by the name of Nationalism. The propriety of the name lies in the claim that the system in question is the logical outworking and development of the germinal idea of a nation, which is that of a union of people for the purpose of using the collective power to promote the common welfare. It is claimed by those who, in this sense, are believers in Nationalism, that this conception of the nation, although at first expressed only by the use of collective power for military and judicial purposes, logically involved, when it should be necessary for the common welfare, a national organization of industry, on the basis of a common obligation of service, and a general guarantee of livelihood. It will be seen that the significance of the word Nationalism, in this sense, quite transcends the merely political or ethical purport of its ordinary sense.

*Reprinted by special permission from The Contemporary Review, London, England.

# EDWARD BELLAMY SPEAKS AGAIN!

In the March number of this Review, M. de Laveleye pursued his criticism of Nationalism by a second article under the title of "Communism." I propose in the present paper to respond to the gist of the criticisms contained in the two articles. I have to thank M. de Laveleye for the very fair statement, as far as it goes, of the industrial aspects of Nationalism, to which he gives a considerable part of the first article. The comment with which he concludes his account of the plan is that there are two principal objections to its practicability— "the first referring to the allotment of functions, the second to the distribution of produce." Under the first head he remarks that obviously, seeing all forms of industry are left open to the election of the workers upon proof of fitness—no other compulsion being used, after the first three years, beyond the requirement that some sort of work should be done—"the pleasanter trades and professions would be taken up, and there would be no one to fill the less agreeable ones."

Of course, the answer to this in the book is that the hours of labour are reduced in the more arduous trades to half, a third, or a quarter of those which are required in the more attractive occupations. M. de Laveleye admits that this principle is certainly just, and might be applied in a certain measure in any national industrial organization, but he thinks there are certain occupations so repulsive, that no comparative reduction of hours consistent with any sort of continuous work would suffice to tempt men to engage in them voluntarily. For examples he instances, among others, the miner's work and the work of stokers on steamships. It does not appear to me that these cases offer any difficulty at all. In the first place, let it be understood that, with the advent of Nationalism, the perilous, insalubrious, and revolting conditions which now quite needlessly involve these and many other forms of labour would be done away with. When the administration has to depend, as it will then have to do, upon volunteers to dig coal, and stoke steamship furnaces, mines will cease to be death-traps, and a part of the money and ingenuity now lavished in making the saloon deck luxurious will be expended in making the stoke hole endurable. When starvation can no longer be depended upon to compel the poor to beg an opportunity to do any sort of work, on any terms, and at any hazard, then, and not a day sooner, will humane and hygienic conditions become universal in industry. Let us suppose the forms of toil instanced by M. de Laveleye to have been thus deprived of their most repulsive features. If it were still found that a reduction of the hours of labour in them, say to three or four a day, were an insufficient inducement to attract volunteers, let us imagine that the length of the vacations given to the miners and stokers were so increased that they had to work but six months out of the year, while the other trades worked, perhaps, ten or eleven. Is it not probable that there would be, under such circumstances, a rush to the mines and steamships which would leave the shops and railways short of help?

But I am not going to let M. de Laveleye off with merely answering his objection. I have a serious counter-charge to make. His argument that society cannot afford to abolish poverty lest men, being no longer threat-

ened with starvation, should be found unwilling to do
the more repulsive sorts of work, is a very explicit argument for human slavery.    Men now living can well remember when this very argument was urged for the retention of slave labour in the sugar-fields of Jamaica, and
the cotton-fields of the Southern United States.    When
Wilberforce and Garrison demanded that the blacks be
set free, it was replied that, if freed, they could no longer
be depended on to cultivate cotton and sugar, and the
world would be left without these products.    Is not this
precisely M. de Laveleye's logic when he reasons that
white men ought not be released from the pressure of
want, lest we should run short of coal, or our steamships
cease to break records?    Could there conceivably be a
stronger argument against the present industrial system
than this deliberate statement by one of its champions
that its successful working demands the retention of a
race of Helots in a state of involuntary servitude?

Next to the difficulty in getting the world's dirty work
done without the lash of hunger, M. de Laveleye declares
the chief objection to Nationalism to be the system of remuneration, that is to say, the equality with which all
share in the total product.    To prove that no industrial
system can succeed in which equality of shares is the
rule, he instances the failure of Louis Blanc's national
workshops at Paris in 1848, and of Marshall Bugeaud's
colonies at Beni-Mered in Algeria.    If he would like a
few dozen more examples of the failure of colonies or
communities established as social or industrial experiments in the midst of incongruous and hostile environ-
ments, I can easily furnish him with them.    Such under-

takings must usually fail for obvious reasons, and even when occasionally they succeed, their success proves as little for their theories as the failure would have proved against them. If I had suggested a colony, these illustrations would be pertinent, but, as it is, I fail to see that they are so. National cooperation is my proposal, nor would any Nationalist suggest that the substitution of the new system for the old should be, as to equality of compensation, any more than as to other details, anything but gradual.

Further representing the impracticability of an industrial system under which all share alike, M. de Laveleye inquires what punishment is to overtake the idler, or the man refusing to work. That compulsion as to work of some sort and punishment for recalcitrancy is contemplated by the plan, he recognizes, but asks who is to apply it, or judge when it is necessary. He says: "Certainly men would in all probability rarely refuse to do any work at all; but those who do as little as possible, or do it badly, are they to be punished or to receive the same salary, or rather to be credited with the same amount, as the others? The State could not send away a bad workman as it can do now, for, there being no private enterprises, this dismissal would be equivalent to capital punishment."

Let me assure M. de Laveleye that the State would not send away a bad workman for quite another reason than that it would be equivalent to capital punishment. The other reason is that so to dismiss him would be to release him from his duty of service. Under the present system of industry, if a man will not work for his living, he is permitted to go his ways, and thenceforth beg or steal it. Under Nationalism a very different course would be pursued. The man who, being able to work, persistently refused to work, would not, as now, be turned loose to prey on the community, but would be made to work in institutions and under discipline prepared for such cases. Today, the loafer may find in the injustices of society many fine pleas for idleness; then, he would be stripped of all, and stand forth self-confessed, a would-be robber and forager on others, to be dealt with as such.

To speak in detail of the penalties by which idleness, disobedience of orders, neglect of duty, and other minor infractions of discipline should be punished, would scarcely be in keeping with an outline discussion like this; but suppose that, besides loss of promotion and its privileges, a temporary increase of work hours, or a severer sort of work, were imposed upon offenders. Is there any doubt that such a punitive system would prove far more effective against neglects of industrial duty than, for example, the system of fines now does in preventing the minor offenses against society?

As to who should judge of the worker's idleness or neglect of duty, that would doubtless be, as judging is now-a-days, a question of evidence for tribunals existing for the purpose. It appears to me that the difficulties M. de Laveleye sees here are not real.

It will be observed that the objections to which I have been endeavoring to reply, intimate in the critic's mind a probable inefficiency in the disciplinary and coercive powers of the administration under the National plan. In his second article, published in the March Contemporary, he abandons this ground and dwells strongly upon the excessive severity and iron rigidity likely to character- ize the proposed industrial regime. Commenting upon this point, he observes that "the gaoler would be the pivot of the new state of society." There is, of course, a sense in which the gaol as the *ultima ratio* of the law, the force which gives meaning to the police courts and legislatures, is the pivot of all society. If it were the pivot of the new society it could only be said that in this respect, it would strikingly resemble the present society. There is, however, a very obvious and conclusive reason for believ- ing that the force of public opinion under the new so- ciety would make the gaoler's duties very light, so far as concerns the punishment of men refusing or neglecting industrial duty. The adventurer who lives by his wits now-a-days, scorning honest labour, is a hero and a fine fellow among his set, and, so long as he avoids open law- breaking, is tolerated by society. Upon reflection, of course, every one is bound to admit that he who does not labour lives at the expense of those who do; but the relations of production with distribution are so complex and fortuitous under the present system that this is only true generally and not particularly. Under the plan of National cooperation the case would, however, be per- fectly clear. As already said, the man able to work and attempting to evade his duty of contributing to the gen- eral produce from which he lived, would be recognized as a thief of the world and a picker of everybody's pocket. There would be no class, no set, no clique in whose eyes such a fellow would be a hero, or anything but a cheat and a cozener—the common enemy of all. It appears to me that, in assuming that the gaoler would be over-worked under the new industrial règime, M. de Laveleye has overlooked this consideration.

Why, even now-a-days, in the better parts of the United States, and I presume in other countries, a man who does not find some regular occupation on coming of age, is, under ordinary circumstances, an object of such general contempt that he must be exceptionally thick-skinned to be able to take comfort in his leisure. How much more would this be true if, as under the plan of National co-operation, the man who shirked his work was recognized as a burden upon the country and upon every one of his neighbors?

Perhaps enough has been said to indicate that the disciplinary and punitive side, the teeth and claws, of the new règime might probably be depended upon to prove efficient in case of need. But while it is requisite to provide society with due facilities for controlling the unruly and mutinous element which is found in all communities, vastly more important is the question of incentives to be offered to that vast majority who are well disposed and ready to do their duty upon reasonable inducement. While Nationalism will undertake to do more than any other règime ever before attempted in compelling the laziest to at least support himself, no system can make much profit out of unwilling workers. No form of compulsion, even if practicable, could take the place of zeal and ambition on the part of the worker, and if the proposed system should fail to stimulate voluntary diligence, it would be of little value that it prevented. outright idleness. What inducement then, does

Nationalism offer to lead a worker to do his best, seeing that all workers, not distinctly negligent, are to fare alike? That is to say, admitting that complete idleness will be effectually prevented, how is zeal in the service to be encouraged? For, without that, there can be no healthy or wealthy industrial state. On this point M. de Laveleye says:

"When remuneration is in proportion to the work accomplished, diligence and activity are encouraged, whereas an equal rate of wages is a premium on idleness. 'But,' argues Mr. Bellamy, 'honour is a sufficient reward in itself, for men will sacrifice everything, even their lives, for it.' It is perfectly true that honour has inspired the most sublime acts and heroic deeds which have called forth universal admiration; but honour can never become the motive power of work or the mainspring of industry. It will not conquer selfish instincts, or overcome instinctive repugnance to certain categories of labour, or the dislike to the wearing monotony of the daily task. It may make a hero, but not a workman."

Here I must beg leave to differ most emphatically from M. de Laveleye. Honour does make a workman as well as a hero, and it is as essential to the make-up of one as the other. This is a matter of common observation, and every man and woman who reads these lines is able to judge between M. de Laveleye and myself on the issue raised. Upon it I am ready to test the whole case of Nationalism, and appeal to the country. I know that in America, at least, the workman who does not carry the feeling of honour into the performance of his task is not worth his salt, and I shall be slow

81

to believe it otherwise in England. So utterly wrong is M. de Laveleye on this point that, so far as there is any good and honest work done under this most ill-jointed system of industry, it is because the sentiment of honour, fast disappearing from the world of commerce and finance, still lingers in the workshop.

Of the motives which spur the well-disposed to diligence under the system of Nationalism, three general classes may be mentioned: First, the sense of honourable and moral obligation to do one's duty, a sentiment which may be expected to develop great influence under a system based, as no other ever has been, upon justice and fair-play for all. Second, the love of approbation, the desire to be thought well of, and to be admired by one's fellow men and women. This sentiment has, no doubt, in all ages and among all races, been on the whole the most powerful, constant, and universal of human motives. It is to-day, and always has been the motive at the bottom of the greater part of that zeal in business and industry which is ascribed, by superficial observers, to love of money. Under Nationalism, when diligence will be public service, and not mere self-service as now, the approbation of the community will attend it and crown it as never before. Even now the able business man and the clever workman are admired by the community, although they are only good to themselves. How much stronger, warmer, and more inspiring that admiration will be under Nationalism when the able manager and skillful artisan will be looked upon as the direct benefactors of all their fellow-citizens!

The third class of motives which will inspire diligence

under Nationalism will be the desire of power, authority, and public station, the wish to lead and direct instead of being led and directed. Let us suppose a system of industry under which superior diligence and excellence of achievement should not only secure various immediate and minor advantages of preference and privilege, but should offer the sure and single way to all positions of authority, of official rank, of civic honour, and of social distinction, of which the express purpose indeed should be to open the career to talent as it never was opened in human affairs before, in order that the strongest and ablest among the people might find themselves at the head of the nation!

Under such a règime, it appears to me highly improbable that the equal provision made for the needs of all will diminish the disposition of men to do their best, but, on the contrary, altogether likely that it will be greatly intensified, in comparison with anything we see today.

I have gone thus explicitly into the motives to diligence under Nationalism for the benefit of candid readers, and not as a response really called for by M. de Laveleye's argument. So far as concerns the merit of his contention that the rule of equal wages is an impracticable one, the simplest and most conclusive way of disposing of that is, no doubt, to refer him to the fact that a large, if not the largest, part of the world's work is at present being done on the basis of standard rates of wages. There are, of course, many industries in which the rule of piece-work prevails, and many sorts of employment in which the rate of pay is settled as to each individual by haggling with the employer, but there are,

# EDWARD BELLAMY SPEAKS AGAIN!

I think, many more (though the precise proportion is immaterial), both of the unskilled and skilled occupations, in which the wages of the worker are determined not by his particular merits, but by the custom of the locality or by a fixed rule of the trade. There is, then, no question as to whether the rule of equal wages will work; it does work.

The standard of wages in different trades does indeed differ, and the pay of foremen and bosses is more than that of the men. It is not, of course, claimed that the Nationalist principle of equality is anywhere as yet fully carried out. It is claimed that in a large proportion of industrial occupations the rank and file of the workers receive a fixed and equal rate of wages, not dependent on personal efficiency, and that this plan is found, as a matter of practical experience, to work satisfactorily.

I wish to call particular attention to the fact that in proportion as trades become highly organized, they tend to adopt the uniform rate of wages. Not to recognize in this tendency one of the lines of the evolution towards the Nationalist principle of a uniform maintenance for all, is to miss a sign of the times so plain that it would seem "a wayfaring man, though a fool, need not err therein." The method of this particular line of evolution will appear as we consider why the members of a trade are moved to adopt the uniform rate of wages. It is simply because the integrity and harmony of the Trade Union, and its consequent ability to provide for its members, require a unity of sentiment and interest on the part of all, and this unity cannot be secured except on the basis of a uniform wage. The cleverer worker knows that in accepting the same wage with the less clever he relatively loses something. But he recognizes that the common gain which he, together with his fellows, derives from the greater efficiency of the union more than compensates him. He has, in a word, learned by hard knocks the wisdom of unselfishness and the bad policy of a too narrow individualism. When, in the progress toward National co-operation, there shall be a question of an organization inclusive of different trades, and ultimately of one including all trades, precisely the same necessity of an identity of feeling and of interest on the part .of the different groups of workers, if the organization is to hold together, will necessitate uniformity of wages in all trades alike, the less attractive being equalized with the more attractive by differences of hours. Any attempt to realize a co-operative commonwealth on any other basis will infallibly fail by the dissensions and mutual jealousies of the trades. It is true that Nationalism goes beyond this, and proposes that the idea of wages be dropped entirely, and the principle of an equal maintenance for all, whether able to work or not, provided all are required to work who are able, be adopted. This, however, is but one step further in the evolution of the same idea which already leads the cleverer worker to consent to an equalization with the less clever in the assurance of a greater ultimate gain. The weak, the sick, and those unable to work for whatever reason, including a large proportion of women, have to be and always have been supported, and often luxuriously supported, out of the earnings of the strong and able. By the rule of an equal maintenance for all, this support would merely be averaged and systematized, its total cost not necessarily being at all increased, while the gain in industrial efficiency by the sense of a complete solidarity of interest among the people, and the impassioned public spirit springing from it, would be incalculable.

It may be well enough to observe just here that the argument for a national co-operative system on the basis of equal material conditions for all, is at all points a twofold argument, moral and economical. It is not only asserted by Nationalists that such an equality would be just even if it were not profitable, but quite as strongly that it would be profitable even if it were not demanded by justice. In this respect Nationalism is like the stork. It not only has two legs, but can stand indefinitely on either.

For the benefit of those whose self-respect might fail to supply a sufficient motive for veracity, Benjamin Franklin invented the maxim, "Honesty is the best policy." For the benefit of persons habituated to consider their fellow-men chiefly with a view to the profit to be made out of them, it should constantly be kept in view that in a strictly business sense "Fraternity is the best policy."

M. de Laveleye is kind enough to say that a system, "very similar to that of Mr. Bellamy," has been known to work very well—for instance, in Peru under the Incas, and in the Paraguay missions of the Jesuits. The ancient civilization of the Incas, as the only record of anything like an organization of industry on a national scale, is indeed profoundly worthy of study, but in referring to it as a system very similar to that of Nationalism, M. de Laveleye is rather out of the way. The Peruvian system, like the Paraguayan system, was the perfect flower of benevolent despotism, while Nationalism will be the consummation of the doctrine of democratic equality, the translation into industrial and economic terms of the equal rights idea, hitherto expressed in terms of politics only. It is hard to see how a contrast can be more antipodal. The Peruvian and the Jesuit systems illustrate the utmost that could be accomplished for human welfare by the paternal principle in Government; Nationalism will undertake to show what can be accomplished by the fraternal principle. The contrast is, in a word, between paternalism and fraternalism, between despotism and equality. Could anything be more complete?

As to M. de Laveleye's second paper appearing in the March number of this REVIEW, I doubt if I ought to reply to it at all, for the reason that, in a strict sense, it does not concern me or my contention. I should have read it through without a suspicion that the writer was criticizing any ideas which I had ever entertained, were it not that he implicates me by name. He begins with a brief general account of pretty nearly all the remarkable social theories and experiments from Plato to these days. He includes in the list societies based upon the community of wives and upon celibacy, upon the Word of God and the Denial of God, the Christian Communism of the early disciples and the Naturalism of Rousseau; the slave-based military system of Sparta, and the modern ideal of social and industrial equality, the military and religious brotherhoods of the Middle Ages, the Jesuitism of Loyola, and the Shakerism of Mother Ann Lee.

The adherents of these apparently very diverse and inconsistent ideals and aspirations, are, he says, in fact all alike, all communists; and he proceeds to argue that what is true of any one of these reformers or their plans is true of all. In this collection M. de Laveleye includes Nationalism as set forth in "Looking Backward."

No doubt I ought to be pleased with a process which lumps me with Plato, and so I should be if in the exceedingly "composite photograph," to which I am permitted to contribute, I were able to detect any trace of my own features or expression.

Recognizing apparently that he has a large generalization on his hands, M. de Laveleye goes on to divide his alleged "communists" into two classes; those who believe in fraternity and those who believe in equality. In common, as I supposed, with most people, I have been in the habit of regarding fraternity and equality as having a very close connection. I have regarded, in fact, fraternity as the flower of equality, and equality as the soil of fraternity. M. de Laveleye says, however, that not only are these ideas not inseparable, but that they are opposed; that there is a gulf fixed between them. The "communists" who base their creed upon fraternity, according to him, are idealists too good for this world, while the "communists" who base their creed upon equality are materialists, too gross for this world, and between the two there can be no compromise. Thus on the principle pursued so successfully in the domestic sphere by Jack Sprat and his wife, he very easily disposes of the whole business of social reform as hitherto advocated, and clears the field for a Utopia of his own—for M. de Laveleye has a Utopia.

Before paying my respects to that, however, there are one or two points to be gathered up.  It is probably not worth while to take up space with a defense of "Looking Backward" from the charge of advocating a community of wives, compulsory atheism, and the general abolition of moral distinctions.  Although M. de Laveleye, by very direct implication, charges me with these and many more offenses, I recognize that he does not really mean it.  I am but the victim of a grand generalization, and it would no doubt be in bad taste to insist that a fine period should be sacrificed for the sake of an individual more or less.

I find one place, however, in the course of this essay on Communism where my critic raises an issue sufficiently direct and definite to be met.  This is where he says that "Mr. Bellamy and communists of his stamp base their systems on the maxim, From each according to his strength; to each according to his wants."  I don't know anything about "communists of his stamp;" it would be too large a contract to undertake to vouch for a class, which, according to M. de Laveleye, includes pretty nearly everybody in the reform line for 2,500 years.  Mr. Bellamy, however, most certainly says no such thing as he is here declared to say.

If by the expression, "from each according to his strength," is meant merely that men ought, as a matter of honour and moral obligation, to regard their strength as the measure of their duty, and weakness and need as sacred titles to their service, I should be sorry to think M. de Laveleye so far differed from moralists in general as to deny it. But if he means, as he certainly seems to say, that this law is laid down by me, not merely as morally obligatory upon the individual, but as a practical basis for determining varying degrees of service to be exacted from individuals and varying degrees of consumption to be permitted to individuals, he is very far astray indeed. Instead of the maxim "From each according to his strength, to each according to his wants," the maxim of Nationalism is "from each equally, to each equally." Instead of an uncertain and unascertainable standard of service, varying with individuals, the service is limited to a fixed and equal term, precisely as is the period of military service in countries where it is universally obligatory. On the other hand, instead of an unregulated or varying consumption being permitted, the credit allotted to all as a means of support is equal and the same, and may not be exceeded. Surely here in neither respect is anything vague or uncertain. It would be interesting to know on what ground M. de Laveleye would justify so complete a misstatement as this on a point which he particularly declares to be vital to the definition of Communism on which his entire argument is based.

This is a suitable point at which to correct an impression which M. de Laveleye seems to have formed that the provision for an equal rate of income for all citizens in some way involves what he calls "a national pot-au-feu, a sort of enforced mess for all time." Does he mean to risk his reputation as a political economist on the state-

90

ment that because groups of workers are paid the same wages, they must necessarily mess together, or that they ordinarily do so, or that they apparently feel any inclination to do so? I have observed no such tendency in the United States under the present industrial system, and I am at a loss for any reason why it should appear under Nationalism, as I understand it. Under national co-operation the same amount of credit as means of support will be guaranteed to all citizens in good standing, from the President to the weakest worker and the person exempt from all work on account of physical disability. This will be done on the ground that their bodily needs are in a large view equal and common, and because their common humanity, and common heirship of the heritage of the race, should overbear all personal considerations in the allotment of the produce of the common inheritance. But while the means of livelihood for all are equal, the manner of the expenditure of these means will rest as absolutely with the individual as does the expenditure of his wages today. The gourmand who spends his income on his table, and the coxcomb who spends it on his back, will find in Nationalism nothing whatever to interfere with the continued indulgence of their idiosyncrasies.

It is rather too bad to have to take up space with statements so obvious as this, but so long as reputable writers continue to assure the public that any real improvement in industrial conditions involves a community of wives, a formal profession of atheism, and the eating of black broth in common, it will continue to be necessary to put on file denials which must appear sufficiently superfluous to persons who have taken pains to inform themselves on the subjects under discussion.

I find it a quite unaccountable oversight on M. de Laveleye's part, that, while ransacking ancient history back to Lycurgus and Manco Capac for intimations of Nationalism, he should fail to take notice of the gigantic contemporary illustrations of the possibility of elaborately organizing vast populations for united action to a common end, which are afforded by the military systems of the great European States. To fail to see, in these wonderful examples of what method and order may accomplish in the concentration and direction of national forces, prototypes of the industrial system of the future is, in my opinion, wholly to fail of rightly interpreting one of the most significant of contemporary phenomena. I wish to call attention to the fact that the fundamental principle of the modern military system, as illustrated in Europe, and as theoretically recognized by all nations, is that every man able to do military duty is bound to render it, without respect of persons, on fixed and equal terms. I wish to call attention to the converse fact that while the duty of service from the individual to the nation is exacted only of those able to serve, the inability, however complete, of a citizen does not discharge the nation from the duty of protecting that citizen with the whole power of the State. In other words, the duty to serve depends on the ability to serve, but the right to protection depends solely and merely on citizenship. I call attention to the fact that these two principles are the basic principles of Nationalism as set forth in "Looking Backward," and that Nationalism, therefore, merely involves

the application to the business of national maintenance of
the principles already freely acknowledged and applied in
the business of national protection.

It appears to me that but two questions are left. First:
Is maintenance as important as protection, or, in other
words, is industry as important to a nation's welfare as
war? Second: Are system, harmony, and concert of action likely to be as advantageous in industry as in war?

I think it will be very hard for any intelligent person
to decline to answer these questions affirmatively, even
though expressly warned that this involves conceding the
whole case of nationalism. It is pertinent to observe
that the principle of the duty of universal industrial service, using the word industrial in the broad sense of all
efforts of mind or body is not a new one. It is recognized as a principle of universal ethics, that no one has
a right to live without work. Many persons here and
there have denied that it can ever be the duty of men
to fight; but I do not think it was ever seriously denied
that it is their duty to work. Upon this postulate Nationalism is based. It is but a corollary of the edict of
Eden: "In the sweat of thy face shall thou eat bread."
This edict has been wholly evaded by many, and upon
those who have not been able to evade it it has weighed
most unequally. Nationalism proposes to impose no new
burden, but to systematize and equalize the ancient burden, and thereby greatly lighten it for all alike, through
the economies a more rational system will evolve.

It should be unnecessary, but to avoid possible mis-
apprehension it is perhaps desirable, to point out just
here, that the analogy between the national military or-

ganizations of Europe and the coming armies of industry in no way extends to the details of the organization of the respective bodies. Except as to the principle of a common duty and the desirability of order, of system, of complete cooperation, and of a central oversight and direction, the conditions of industry and those of war are very dissimilar.

There will be no question of any stricter discipline for the members of the army of industry than is customary in any well-conducted industrial establishment today, while, except as to work and in work hours, the citizen will be, in all respects, as much his own master as at present, and, for that matter, much more so.

If one would be assured that it will be safe to depend on men whose motives are sense of duty, the desire of reputation, and ambition for honour, rank, and power, instead of the pursuit of personal gain, to act as captains and generals of industry, and to conduct and administer the business of the people, he has but to visit the offices of the general staff of one of the great European armies, and inspect the departments of the paymaster-general, of the commissariat, of transportation, of engineering and construction, of ordnance and war material, together with the various Government manufacturing establishments which supply the army, as well as the elaborate machinery through which the entire resources of the country are constantly kept in hand and held available for military purposes, though meanwhile employed in peaceful pursuits.

It will be found, I think, that the business of organizing and fully providing for all the needs of a body of men comprising the whole early manhood of a nation, including machinery for utilizing the entire material resources of the country in case of need, involves the constant solution of problems of business administration on a far greater scale than they are presented by the affairs of the largest of industrial or commercial syndicates, and that, as a matter of fact, the work of the epauletted administrators is done with an exactitude and fidelity unequalled in private business. Upon this administrative and essentially business side of the great modern military organizations the advocate of the practicability of Nationalism may properly lay peculiar stress. While in its warlike and strictly martial aspects the modern European army shows striking general analogies to the proposed National industrial organization, when we come to the business administration of its affairs, we see tasks performed, and a routine of duties discharged, not only analogous to, but, to a considerable extent, identical with, those which Nationalism will lay upon the State.

And now we come to M. de Laveleye's own Utopia. While condemning as unprofitable and undesirable all plans of social reform based upon the principles of fraternity and equality, or recognizing any sort of community of interest among men, or making any account of duty or honour as motives, except in connection with blood letting, he nevertheless recognizes that the advocates of reform have some excuse in the unquestionable evils of existing industrial conditions. He admits that there is need of reform, and proceeds to state the principle on which alone he considers it to be possible or desirable, as follows: "The fundamental precept of social economy should be: To each worker his produce, his entire produce and nothing but his produce. The great problem of social organization is to realize this formula of justice. If this were once applied, pauperism and divitism, misery and idleness, vice and spoliation, pride and servitude, would disappear as by magic from our midst."

In closing his argument, he reiterates this maxim as at once "the absolute negation of communism and the most sacred justice," and predicts that it will receive due legislative recognition.

I am sorry to differ so completely as I am obliged to from this conclusion. It is my own belief that the maxim above stated will never be recognized by legislation, for the reason that its practical application is rendered impossible by the nature of things, and that this attempt to apply it, while totally failing to effect the reforms promised, would incidentally involve a repudiation of some of the main ethical ideas of the race, together with the complete abandonment of the industrial methods which distinguish civilization from savagedom and have chiefly created modern wealth.

To take up the moral aspect of the maxim first, it will be observed that if the producer is to have "his entire produce, and nothing but his produce" there will obviously be nothing left for the non-producer, and for the weak producer only a pittance. This shuts out entirely, or reduces to the crumbs and crusts of the table, women, children, the aged, the infirm, and those crippled by disease and accident, or defective by nature. All these would exist only by the favour of the strong and healthy men

96

of working age. So long, indeed, as women were unencumbered with children their labour might well avail for a bare support; but not for the comforts at all corresponding to those enjoyed by men. For any share in these they must depend on masculine favour or charity. Let it be observed that this result of the application of M. de Laveleye's maxim would involve on the part of all these classes a far more abject state of dependence than they now are in, for, at present, much of the world's wealth is not, as he would have it, limited to the producer, but is in the hands of non-workers. This arrangement the application of the maxim would abolish, with the result of bringing all non-workers or feeble workers into that relation of direct and complete dependence upon the favour of the stronger members of the community which characterizes the savage state. Of course, the stronger might, if so disposed, provide for the weaker; but, under the maxim, the weaker would have no right or recognized claim to any provision beyond what they could make for themselves. And this is the arrangement under which, we are told, "pauperism and misery," "pride and servitude would disappear as by magic from our midst." Certainly it would be a clear case of magic if they should disappear under a system apparently expressly adapted to promote, legitimatize and perpetuate them.

Let us for a moment consider the ethical quality of this proposition with particular reference to the way it would affect the condition of woman. For the sake of the race, Nature has laid upon woman burdens which disqualify her, in comparison with man, as a producer.

# EDWARD BELLAMY SPEAKS AGAIN!

On account of this disqualification, resulting from her consecration to the interests of humanity, it is proposed to put her on half allowance, and leave her to beg and wheedle for the rest of her needs. That is to say, her weakness, which in view of its cause would, one would suppose, among any race of intelligent beings, be held to constitute the most sacred of titles to all things the powers of the race could command, is made the excuse for adding to the burden she already bears for man, the indignity of personal dependence upon his favour for her maintenance. It appears to me, and I think will appear to most men who have not forgotten that they were born of woman, that what M. de Laveleye calls "the most sacred justice" is in this regard an injustice of which it is difficult to say whether the magnitude or the ineffable meanness is the more striking aspect. It is quite true that since the beginnings of history mankind has utterly failed to recognize the duty of society to secure the freedom and dignity of woman, as Nationalism proposes to do, by guaranteeing her economical independence. The recompense by indignity and oppression of her everlasting martyrdom in behalf of the race has been the great crime of mankind to this day, a crime to the proportions of which the eyes of men are at last beginning to be opened. It is now proposed in this year 1890, that, instead of redressing this ancient wrong, the civilized world shall re-affirm it as the corner-stone of an improved society. I do not think the proposition will prevail.

It is worth considering that, if, indeed, M. de Laveleye's maxim is correct, that every worker should have "his produce, his entire produce, and nothing but his produce," as a matter "of most sacred justice," the legislators of the past two thousand years have been wholly wrong in what has commonly been considered their progressive legislation, for the larger part of this supposed progressive legislation has consisted in successive limitations of the exclusive claims of the producer to his produce, and successive assertions of the claims of non-producers to partake of it. The right of the wife and the child are now fully established, not only as a matter of a mere moral claim, but of legal title, to share in the produce of the husband and father, while, through taxation, the claims of the dependent and destitute classes of all sorts, by no other title than their need and their destitution, to share the wealth of the producer are yearly more fully asserted. For every sort of civil, military, educational, and miscellaneous, common and public purposes, the producer is constantly being mulcted of his produce, and the more civilized the nation the less is his "sacred" title to that produce recognized. Instead of regarding the individual man as absolutely without duties, natural or social, without responsibility to past, present, or future, as the maxim under consideration presupposes him, the constant tendency of civilization has been in the direction of imposing upon him ever new duties, tributes, and responsibilities towards society in general, and especially towards its weaker and unproductive classes, as well as in the interests of any and all undertakings tending to promote the general welfare or avert the general damage. Nationalism is the logical evolution of this tendency. M. de Laveleye's plan, on the other hand, contemplates its reversal. The issue between us is in a nutshell: M. de Laveleye is a revolutionist; I am an evolutionist. Merely as to the question of practicability, in order to establish M. de Laveleye's system, a dozen laws would have to be repealed to every new one which Nationalism would require to be enacted.

But let me not be charged with giving a one-sided consideration, too largely tinged with sentiment, to M. de Laveleye's Utopia. Let us look at its economical aspect. Let us imagine that, intoxicated by the vision of a society illustrating and embodying unmitigated selfishness, the world had resolved to repeal all the humane legislation of the past two thousand years and reorganize upon the maxim, "to the worker his produce, his entire produce, and nothing but his produce." Let us see what, if any, philosophical and practical difficulties would be likely to arise. If Shylock must have his pound of flesh, let us see that he takes no more than the letter of the bond.

To begin at the beginning: If a man be entitled to "nothing but his produce," by what title shall he claim ownership of himself and the consequent right to use his powers for his own benefit? That this is no fanciful objection will appear when we reflect that, under the ancient civilizations and today in barbarous countries, parents were and are held to be, by the most sacred of titles, absolute proprietors of their sons and daughters, and certainly, if M. de Laveleye's maxim were ethically sound, they ought to be, for no production is so painful, so costly, and so anxious as to the production and nurture of human beings. M. de Laveleye's maxim appears logically to require the re-introduction of the patriarchal system.

In the second place, if the worker, as a matter of "most sacred justice" is entitled to his produce and "nothing but his produce," by what possible title shall he venture to appropriate any part of the earth and its natural resources, seeing that manifestly he did not produce them? And yet, if he does not appropriate them, it is certain that he can produce nothing at all or even find a place to stand on. It appears that, as a preliminary to the proposed plan of apportionment, the whole question of the terms on which men should use this earth and its resources would have to be adjusted, a question which, it is needless to observe, opens up the entire subject of sociology. In view of this consideration, it cannot be said that M. de Laveleye's maxim offers what may be called a short cut to the social solution.

But, for the sake of argument, let us suppose these two rather large difficulties to have been in some way gotten over and proceed to consider some practical inconveniences which would appear in the application of the maxim to the world's business.

Obviously, if every worker's holding is to be his produce and "nothing but his produce," he must not have the use of inherited wealth in any form. The right of inheritance must therefore be abolished. But who is to take the estates of the dying? Under M. de Laveleye's rule they go neither to the heirs nor are held in common. They must apparently be burned.

Again, although the worker, under Mr. de Laveleye's

maxim, may accumulate and use capital which is self-produced, he may not rent or borrow or lend with or without interest, for the interest, or the use, would be, to lender or borrower respectively, something other than his own produce. And, again, he could not employ anyone or have assistants of any sort by whom he made a profit, for this profit would plainly be something beside his own produce. By the same rule, he could not go into partnership or any form of co-operation with anybody, for, whenever the labour of two men is blended, their produce is intermingled, and then it is impossible to make sure that each has "his produce, his entire produce, and nothing but his produce." In cases of co-operation some arbitrary plan of division has to be agreed upon, halves, quarters, thirds, or something else, but any such method would fatally offend M. de Laveleye's ideal of "most sacred justice." As for the modern system of complex interdependence and subdivision of work, by which the individual worker performs a single process, perhaps, out of a score requisite to complete the product—a system from which the wealth of the modern world largely results—that, of course, would have to be given up and a return made to the old style of independent and wholly individual production, whereby, with inconceivable waste of effort, each worker wholly completed his own product and then took it to market. Indeed, that it might be even approximately possible to determine the precise product of each worker, as sharply distinguished from that of every other, it would be practically necessary that every worker should be isolated. Even then the propensity of men to help one another is so strong, that, until the com-

munity should be educated up to M. de Laveleye's standard of "sacred justice," it would be highly desirable that
a policeman should be assigned to each worker to prevent
the surreptitious exchange of assistance. By the time
this point had been reached in preparing for the ideal
system of distributing human produce, it is to be feared
there would not be any produce, worth speaking of, left
to distribute.

And yet even at this stage the process of stripping the
individual of all advantages not self-derived, which
would be necessary to make sure that he received "nothing but his produce," would be by no means completed.
It is a serious thing for the individual to call for an account and trial balance between himself and his race, as
M. de Laveleye's maxim in effect does. All that a man
produces today more than did his cave-dwelling ancestor,
he produces by virtue of the accumulated achievements,
inventions and improvements of the intervening generations, together with the social and industrial machinery
which is their legacy. All these, of which the sum is civilization, are the common inheritance of the race, the
capital of society. Its elements have not descended to us
by any individual or traceable line, and cannot be claimed
by an individual, but only by a common and social title.
For the heritage of civilization the individual is the debt-
or of mankind; for its use humanity is his creditor; to it
he has no claim save under the perpetual tribute of social
duty. Nine hundred and ninety-nine parts out of the
thousand of every man's produce are the result of his
social inheritance and environment. The remaining part
would probably be a liberal estimate of what by "sacred

justice" could be allotted him as "his product, his entire product, and nothing but his product."

In view of the foregoing considerations there appears to be no escape from the following conclusions: The affairs of men, as the result of an indefinite period of gregarious life, have become so involved as to be inextricable. Even though, in order to disentangle them, it were thought worth while to disintegrate the social organism to its ultimate particles, and unravel to the last thread the fabric of civilization, yet would the sacrifice avail nothing, for even then the earth and its resources, to which men can have no title unless it be a common one, would remain the basis of all production.

The human heritage must, therefore, be construed, and can only be construed, as an estate in common, essentially indivisible, to which all human beings are equal heirs. Hitherto this community and equality of right have been disregarded, the heirs being left to scramble and fight for what they could individually get and keep. Thanks to the growth of human intelligence, a world in revolt testifies today that this insane injustice is to be suffered no longer. Unless humanity be destined to pass under some at present inconceivable form of despotism, there is but one issue possible. The world, and everything that is in it, will ere long be recognized as the common property of all, and undertaken and administered for the equal benefit of all. Nationalism is a plan for establishing and carrying on such an administration.

# First Steps Toward Nationalism

## By Edward Bellamy

*(From The Forum, October, 1890\*)*

THE plan of national industrial cooperation, on the basis of general business partnership of all the people for their equal benefit, which has come to be known as nationalism, appears to be regarded by some rather as a theory dealing with the ultimate possibilities of human development than as a proposition tending to immediate action or to practical results. It has, indeed, been spoken of facetiously as a castle in the air, with no ladder to climb up by. It is proposed in the present paper to correct this notion, not only by showing that there is a ladder, but by pointing out the first half-dozen rounds of it, and by indicating the rest. In other words, a brief statement is intended of a few of the measures of practical legislation which nationalists urge as first steps toward realizing their ideal of a complete national industrial partnership.

Stated in general terms, the policy proposed by nationalists is the successive nationalizing or municipalizing of public services and branches of industry, and the simultaneous organization of the employees upon a basis of guaranteed rights, as branches of the civil service of

---

*Reprinted by special permission from The Forum Magazine.

the country; this process being continued until the entire transformation shall have been effected.

I think I am safe in saying that all nationalists agree that the first business to be nationalized should be the telegraph and telephone services. The Constitution of the United States makes it the duty of Congress to establish and to conduct a post office. The business of a post office is to furnish facilities for the transmission of intelligence. At the time the Constitution was adopted, the transmission of intelligence was effected wholly by the carriage of letters; and by providing for the carriage of letters the government discharged its full duty under the Constitution. Since then, electrical invention has rendered the telegraph and the telephone essential and all-important factors in this work. Was it not manifestly the duty of Congress under the Constitution to attach these services to the Post-office Department as soon as they were found necessary adjuncts to the business of that department? This, however, has not been done; and, by failing therein, the post-office service has fallen behind the world's progress and has become relatively a less complete and efficient organization, for the purposes of its establishment, than it was a hundred years ago. At that time the post office provided the people with complete facilities for the transmission of intelligence; at present it provides only partial facilities for that purpose, leaving the people to supply its deficiencies, if they can, by bargaining with private corporations, whose cheapest rates are rarely less than several times what a national service would need to charge. The matter of the precise amount of exorbitance on the part of

106

the corporations which supply the deficiencies of the post office, is not, however, material to the present contention, which is that, even if the service could be performed no cheaper by the post office, it is the business of the post office to do it, and that Congress fails to discharge its constitutional duty to maintain a post office so long as it neglects to complete its facilities in accordance with modern standards. It is not merely constitutional to establish a government telegraph; it is unconstitutional not to do so.

It should be understood, moreover, that no sort of plan for employing private corporations through the government to do telegraph work for the people at a profit upon a preposterously-inflated stock, will be accepted by the people in place of a government telegraph service to be conducted by the government, as the present mail service is, at cost. Of course it would be only fair for the government to offer to purchase at a fair appraisal any existing telegraph lines, satisfactory in equipment, which might be offered it; but the country certainly would not consent to an appraisal which should exceed the cost of duplicating such lines. As to the advantages to the people which would result from a government telegraph service, it is sufficient to refer to the fact that the corporation which at present does nearly all the telegraph business of the country, pays out of its profits a good interest on a capital about four times as great as the expenditure which would be required to duplicate the entire plant, the latter figure being admittedly less than twenty million dollars. The government telegraph service could then be furnished at one-fourth the cost of the present service, even assuming that the same interest would be paid on the investment, which is an unnecessary assumption, as there would be no need to issue bonds for the small sum required to buy or to build the lines.

To all or any objections to the advantages of a government telegraph, the example of Great Britain alone, not to speak of the many other countries which have adopted it, is an answer so absolute and conclusive as to render any other superfluous. The British people are more like ours than any other, and certainly in love of liberty and hatred of officialism they are quite equal to Americans. They find, however, that government telegraphy is so far superior to their former private facilities, as well as so much cheaper, that any proposition to return to the latter would be laughed at in England.

Another extension of the present post office business which is advocated by nationalists, as necessary to bring it up to the degree of efficiency attained in other countries, relates to the establishment of a parcel-express service. The transportation of parcels is a recognized part of the business of the post office in this country as in others. Hitherto, however, the limitations as to size, and otherwise, upon parcels, with the absurd idea of adapting them to the capacity of mail bags, have rendered this service of very small utility to the people, compared with what it easily might be, and with what it is in other countries. It is proposed that the existing provisions for the transport of parcels be so extended as to furnish the people with an adequate express service at cost, thereby relieving them of the necessity of paying high rates for such service to private corporations. The expense connected with this extension would be very trifling.

Thirdly, nationalists are in complete agreement as to the desirability of an immediate national assumption of control over the railroads of the country. The constitutional warrant for this action is perfectly obvious under the clause which gives Congress power to "regulate commerce with foreign nations and among the several States." The only question that there is room for, under this clause, is as to the extent to which government control must be asserted in order to regulate such commerce in a satisfactory manner. By the interstate commerce law, Congress has, very late in the day indeed, but at last, committed itself to the performance of this constitutional duty. The most important result of that law has been, however, not what it has accomplished, but what it has failed to accomplish; that is to say, the practical demonstration it has given that no regulation can be effectual which stops short of full control. It may be observed in passing, that even if the clause of the Constitution referred to did not, as it does, authorize government management of railroads, that power would be found in the clause giving Congress authority to "establish post roads." Will anyone maintain that a dirt road is an adequate and exclusive definition of a post road, in these days when ninety-nine hundredths of all mail matter is carried by railroads?

The construction of the words of the constitutional clause referred to—"commerce . . . among the several states"—so as to limit congressional control to railroads which cross State boundaries, is absurd. The fact, for example, that the line of the New York Central Railroad does not enter Massachusetts, in no way renders it less necessary to commerce between the people of central New York and those of Massachusetts. Is it to be supposed that the Constitution intended Congress to regulate commerce for the benefit exclusively of people living on the State borders and not also for the benefit of those living in the interiors of States? Is it probable that the power conferred on Congress was intended to be so limited as to enable corporations controlling highways to nullify it by the simple device of changing the names and nominal ownership of such highways at State lines?

Public control of the railroads, it should be remembered, is merely the application to iron roads of a principle long ago fully recognized and now universally applied to wagon roads in general, and to bridges. Formerly a considerable part of these highways, then the only means of commerce, were owned by private companies, which made a profit by tolls on travel and traffic. With the growth of more intelligent and more liberal ideas of public policy, everyone recognized that the general interests of communities do not permit their means of intercourse to be privately owned, and to be taxed for private profit. As a result of this conviction, nearly all privately-owned highways and bridges have now been made public property. Meanwhile, however, the intent of this wise and liberal policy, which was to free commerce from private exactions, has been completely frustrated by the progress of invention, and by the failure of legislation to keep pace with it—as in the relations of the post office and the telegraph. While our com-

110

munities have been buying up and making public the wagon roads and bridges of the country, commerce has been forsaking them more and more completely for the railroads. The result today is that the justly-condemned and rejected principle of private ownership and taxation of the means of commercial intercourse has become more absolutely dominant than ever. Either the people of this country have made a mistake in liberating the turnpikes and the bridges from private taxation, and ought to put the toll-gates back, or else they stand committed to the policy of public control of the railroads.

There is a difference of opinion as to the desirability of free trade with foreign nations, but surely there can be but one opinion as to the desirability of free trade within the Union. It is strange that men who work themselves into a fever over the iniquity of taxing in the slightest degree our trade with foreign nations, even though the tax goes into the public treasury and is levied in the name of the public interest, should see nothing objectionable in the taxation of domestic trade, by private persons, at private caprice, for private profit. It appears to me necessary only for the people to see this matter in its true light, to bring about a practical unanimity of opinion in favor of the nationalist idea of free trade between the States, and of the acceptance of the nationalist plan for securing it, namely, a national railroad service to be run at cost and not for profit.

It is conceivable, indeed, that the railroad corporations might exercise their power over the commerce of the country with such moderation and judgment as to induce the people to wink at the danger and absurdity of leaving such a power to private persons. In the actual case, however, no such plea for tolerating the corporate control of railroads can possibly be advanced. The tolls charged by the railroads are universally exorbitant—a fact necessarily resulting from the attempt to pay the largest possible interest upon capitalizations which, whether owing to corrupt or wasteful methods of construction, to excessive stock-watering, or to both, are greatly in excess of the actual value of the roads. Not only are the charges exorbitant, but the treatment of the public by the managements is, in a large proportion of cases, capricious, vexatious, overbearing, and arbitrary.

In view of recent events, it is timely to observe that the national control of railways is the only way by which the travel and traffic of the country can be saved from constant interruption as the result of quarrels between the corporations and their employees. National control, on the one hand, would be based, as hereafter explained, upon the guaranteed rights of employees; and the force of public opinion, informed by the perfect publicity of the management and acting directly through Congress, would insure their just and humane treatment and the redress of grievances. On the other hand, the power of the nation would guarantee the public at large against any forcible interference with the railroad lines. It is preposterous that so vast and so vital a national interest as the railroad service should be dependent upon the maintenance of a good understanding between irresponsible groups of capitalists and their employees.

A consideration which, even in default of all other arguments, would be conclusive in favor of national control of the railroads, remains to be mentioned. Indeed, it scarcely needs mention, so present is it to the minds of thinking Americans in these days. I refer, of course, to the demoralizing effect upon our politics of the vast money power of the railroads and of its unprincipled use to control legislation. The experience and observation of every reader will, I think, bear me out in saying that it would be difficult to exaggerate the magnitude and the peril of this abuse. The railroad corporations and syndicates are subjects at once too powerful and too unscrupulous for the safety of the Republic.

As to the method of nationalizing railroads, various opinions may be held. At present, my own is that the purchase of the roads outright would be uncalled for and unwise, and that the best course would be the assumption of a permanent government control of the system. An analogy for such a control, although of course not a close one, may be found in that already exercised with such admirable success over bankrupt roads by United States receivers. The present security-holders would continue to receive such reasonable dividends, on a just valuation of the plants, as might be earned.

The terms on which the ultimate extinguishment of private title to the roads should be effected, might be left open. Meanwhile it is to be observed that the interests of the security-holders themselves, which are at present so often recklessly or criminally sacrificed by dishonest or speculative directors, or by excessive and blackmailing competition, would be protected by national control, not less than those of the general public. Future railroad construction would, of course, be exclusively by

113

the government. Practical objections to the feasibility of government management are once for all answered by its success in Germany and in other European states, and perhaps still more conclusively in some respects, though on a smaller scale, by the brilliant success of government management in the Australian colony of Victoria, where the form of government is popular, where its methods are partisan, like our own, and where the people themselves are quite as jealous of officialism as are Americans.

Fourthly, nationalists propose immediate legislation looking toward government control of the coal mines of the country. If the corporate control of railroads amounts to a system for enabling private persons to tax the commerce of the country for their private profit, corporate control of the coal mines is in effect a system for enabling private persons to tax the manufactures of the country for their private profit. Coal is a main factor in the cost of manufactures, and in so far as it is not furnished to our manufacturers as cheaply as it could be, they are handicapped in their competition with those of other countries. The real enemies of American manufactures are not the pauper laborers of Europe, but the coal barons of Pennsylvania and Ohio, who by their banded action restrict the production of coal and maintain its price at a preposterous figure. If there is any power in the American people to protect their own interests, they cannot exercise it more wisely than by putting an end to this state of things. I have mentioned only the business argument; but there is a two-fold humane argument for government control of the coal business, which of itself

should suffice.  First, in this climate, coal is a prime
necessity of life, and no nation deserves to be a nation
which will tolerate a needless restriction of its supply
and a heightening of its price for the benefit of a few
men.  Secondly, the inhuman treatment of the coal-min-
ers is an offense to humanity which cries aloud to be
abated.  The following plan is suggested for a national
administration of coal mines.  They should, in the first
place, be continuously worked until the product fully
meets the demand—not at the present artificially-height-
ened price, but at the absolute cost price.  Coal-distrib-
uting centers should be formed throughout the country,
each to supply the communities within a certain radius.
The coal should be forwarded to these centers as fast
as mined, to be thence furnished to consumers as called
for.  As a result of this plan, the supply of coal at hand
would always be ample, transportation would never be
clogged, and the price would not only be the lowest possible cost price, but would not vary between Winter
and Summer, or between warm and cold seasons.  The
price of corn and wheat and potatoes must change according to the capricious bounty of Nature; but the coal
crop is not dependent upon seasons, and, under a rational plan of production and distribution, need not vary in
price.

Fifthly, nationalists everywhere are agitating in favor
of the assumption and conduct by municipalities of local
public services, such as transit, lighting, heating, and the
water supply, which are now rendered by corporations;
and they vehemently oppose the granting of any further
franchises for such purposes.  Even when these bodies

manage such businesses in the cheapest and most honest way possible, the people pay a tax to them equal to the profit the corporations make. In most cases, however, the corporations rendering such services have inflated their capital far beyond the actual value of their plants, and by this inflation the tax paid them by the people in the form of profit is proportionally increased over what it would be under an honest management. In respect to the undertaking of public services by municipalities, our American communities are unaccountably behind those of Europe. Fortunately, a more intelligent public opinion on this subject is rapidly forming among us.

I have referred to the organization of the employee of nationalized or municipalized services as proceeding *pari passu* with the assumption of public control over them. The manner of the organization of this industrial civil service is vital to the plan of nationalism, not only on account of the rights it guarantees to employees, but by its effect to prevent their intimidation or control for political purposes by government. Upon the nationalizing or municipalizing of a business, the employees in it would be taken bodily over into the public service. The force would then be strictly graded, and would be kept up exclusively by admissions to the lowest grade, with subsequent promotions. Admissions would be restricted to persons meeting certain prescribed conditions of fitness strictly adapted to the duties to be discharged, and selections for vacancies would be made from among competent candidates, not by appointment, but either by lot or in order of filed applications. Promotions would be a matter of right, and not of favor, based upon merit as

116

shown by record, combined with a certain length of service, and upon proof of qualifications for the higher rank. No employee would be dismissed except for cause, after a hearing before an impartial tribunal existing for the purpose. Suspension of subordinates pending trial would, of course, be allowed to the management, with full control otherwise of the operations of the force. Support in case of accident, sickness, and age would be guaranteed, to be forfeited only by bad conduct. It is proposed by nationalists that this radical and only effectual plan of civil-service reform be immediately applied to all existing national, state, and municipal services.

Nationalists advocate laws in every State making obligatory the education of children during the whole school year, up to seventeen years, forbidding their employment during the school year, and providing for the assistance, from public funds, of children whose parents are unable to support them during school attendance. It is held by nationalists that the fact that a child's parents are poor, or even thriftless, is no sufficient reason for condemning the child to the life-long serfdom of ignorance, and that it is the duty of the State to see that children are not so condemned.

No doubt the comment upon the foregoing statement of nationalist propositions will be that they are all measures called for by considerations of general public expediency, without reference to nationalism as an ulterior end. Precisely so, and just this, I hope, may be truly said of every subsequent step which nationalists shall advocate. They propose no revolutionary methods, no hasty or ill-considered measures provocative of reaction,

117

no letting go of the old before securing a hold on the new; but an orderly progress, of which each step shall logically follow the last, and shall be justified to the most shortsighted by its immediate motives and results, without invoking any considerations of ultimate ends. Those who wish to go only a step at a time, we welcome as allies, and we pledge them a cooperation which is not the less cordial and considerate because of the fact that results which they regard as ends seem to us but means to ends far greater.

As to the steps of the later stages in the evolution of complete national cooperation, it is unnecessary, and would be presumptuous, to speak positively; but in a purely speculative way a few words may be said about them. When the businesses described shall have been nationalized or muncipalized, there will be a body of nearly two million workers in the public service. Here will be consumers enough to support the beginnings of national productive industries, both manufacturing and agricultural, together with a system of distribution, for the exclusive supply of those in the public service. Such government establishments would produce and distribute, strictly at cost, with an absolute guarantee against adulteration and fraud. In order not to derange the general market, which would continue to be supplied by private establishments working for profit, vouchers of credit at the national stores would be issued only to workers in the national service, in such proportions of their remuneration as they might choose, and goods would be supplied at the national stores for these vouchers only. How long it would take such vouchers to command a pre-

mium over gold, which could purchase only adulterated
and high-priced goods produced for profit by private
persons, may be inferred. With a considerable part of
the nation's workers in the public service, with a system
of agricultural and manufacturing production organized
for their needs, with a complete distributive system, and
with a substitute for money introduced, the completion
of the national cooperative fabric, with its requirement
of service from all and with its guarantee of maintenance to all, upon the basis of equality, would be merely
a question of time. Probably it would require but a
short time, for it is believed that the first successful nationalizing of an important industry would greatly accel-
erate the subsequent steps of the process, by the object
lessons it would afford of the advantages of the new
system, alike to the employees directly affected and to
the community at large.

# Some Misconceptions of Nationalism

## By Edward Bellamy

*(From The Christian Union, November 13, 1890)*

A HOPEFUL sign for Nationalism is the fact that its opponents usually criticize it for what it is not, which suggests the possibility that they may become good Nationalists when they learn what it is. I propose very briefly, as must needs be in a paper of this length, to correct some of these misconceptions.

First. Nationalism is not based on the maxim, To each according to his needs, from each according to his abilities. Of course, as a matter of conscience, every man is bound to do all he can, and the needs of others are sacred claims upon his service; but both abilities and needs are indeterminate, and therefore could not be made the basis of any regulation to be enforced by society. The principle of Nationalism is: From all equally; to all equally. Nationalism will require of all not exempted by natural defect or inability an equal term of industrial service, using this expression as inclusive of all useful mental as well as physical effort. It is, of course, true that men will serve more or less efficiently according to their abilities, just as soldiers in military service do; but the terms of the industrial, as of the military, service, the requirements made of the workers, as of soldiers, will be equal for all. Conversely, the Nation will guarantee to citizens, both workers and those wholly or partially unable to work—strong with weak, women with men, sick with well—an equal maintenance. That is to say, Nationalism adopts the half-truth expressed in the old adage that the world owes every one a living, but not without supplementing it with the other half of the truth —that everyone owes the world a reasonable service. Nationalists argue that it is the business of society to provide the machinery requisite for the discharge of these reciprocal obligations of the community and the individual, and believe that nothing but national co-operation will furnish that machinery.

It is worth consideration that, as between the workers, the provision for an equal maintenance, regardless of differences in personal efficiency, is not a new idea, but only the extension to all trades of the principle of a uniform rate of wages already prevailing by custom or by trade rule in very many occupations, skilled and unskilled. A large proportion of the trades-unions find it necessary to enforce this rule very rigidly as the only way to secure harmony of interest, and consequently of feeling, among the membership of particular trades; and the same consideration, if no other, would render the extension of the same rule to all trades an indispensable condition to the stability of any system of national co-operation.

As to the proposition of Nationalism to extend the guarantee of an equal maintenance, not only to all workers, but to those also who are wholly or partially unable to work, such as the sick, the infirm, and women, this too will be admitted, upon a moment's reflection, to be an innovation in form rather than in substance. The dependent classes now and always have been supported out of the earnings of the workers—some in luxury, some in penury, but all supported in some way. Nationalism will only average and systematize this support, without necessarily increasing the total cost to the workers, while, by abolishing the humiliating personal dependence of the weak and infirm upon the favor of the strong and well for the means of support, it will spare the self-respect of a class already sorely burdened by nature, to the incalculable gain, in dignity and nobility, of human relations.

Second. While Nationalism means that the strong shall bear the infirmities of the weak, it does not mean that the industrious shall support the idle. On the contrary, for the first time in human history, it will take the lazy off the backs of the willing and compel them to support themselves, if not by voluntary labor, then by involuntary.

Third. But, granting the suppression of idleness, will not equality of maintenance on the part of all workers leave less motive to strenuous exertion than the pursuit of wealth now calls forth? The reply is that mutual emulation, the desire of approbation, and the ambition for name and prominence are the real motives which, thinly disguised under the name of love of money, at present prompt the bulk of the world's work, and all its good work. These motives would not only be preserved, but greatly intensified, under Nationalism, which would make the ranks, dignities, offices, and honors, from lowest to highest, of the industrial service and of the State, with the social distinction corresponding to them, exclusively the prizes of superior diligence and achievement. Since all would gain equally by efficiency in the public service, the public interest would imperatively demand that the career should be open to talent as it never had been before.

Fourth. But will not Nationalism discourage individuality? Let us see. At present the vast majority of persons do not receive education enough to find out what their individual qualities and aptitudes are. Even when these are discovered, there is no provision whatever for assisting the individual to secure the sort of work he prefers and is best fitted for. Chance and circumstance determine the fate of most. Warped faculties and stunted growth, round pegs in square holes and square pegs in round ones, are the natural results of these conditions. Finally, the dependence for employment of all workers, manual or intellectual, upon the favor of individuals, corporations, communities, or groups of patrons, makes originality or independence of speech or conduct an indulgence involving the risk of livelihood for one's self and family. Fortunate are the few who have not felt the pressure of this sordid bondage.

Under Nationalism, on the contrary, the universal enjoyment of the best educational advantages might be depended on in the first place to provide opportunity for developing every one's qualities and aptitudes—that is to say, for discovering his individuality. Seeing that under a national co-operative system every person not employed to the best advantage would be a public loss to the extent of the misfit, the utmost pains would be taken, as a measure of economy quite apart from moral motives, to see that every one was helped to the kind of work he was best adapted to. Finally, no one would

be dependent in any way as to livelihood upon the favor
of any individual, group, or community, however large,
but would have his or her maintenance guaranteed by the
constitution of the Nation, not to be diminished or taken
away during orderly behavior by anything less than a
revolution. Could conditions more favorable than these
to the development of a robust individuality be imagined? So far will Nationalism be from discouraging individuality, that it will constitute a school for developing it.

Owing to their dependence for maintenance upon the
favor of men, which again is largely a reflection of public opinion, women are doubly the slaves of convention-
ality, and need to be heroines to assert independence and
individuality. As a consequence of this fact, the moral
and intellectual development of the race has been incal-
culably retarded. By guaranteeing women economical
independence of and equality with men as a corner-stone
of its polity, Nationalism, in the only effectual way possible, will bring to pass the bodily, mental, and moral enfranchisement of woman.

Fifth. An equal provision for maintenance does not
mean a uniform mode of maintenance, or a similar manner of life, any more than the receipt of the same amount
in wages, salary, or income by two or more persons at
the present day means that they must wear the same
clothes, eat the same dishes, or choose the same wall paper. If everybody wants to live like everybody else under Nationalism, of course they will be free to do so, but
there will be no more reason why they should than there
is today.

# EDWARD BELLAMY SPEAKS AGAIN!

Much anxiety has been expressed lest equality of educational advantages and of incomes should make society dull and monotonous. The inference is that the educated, refined, and well-to-do nowadays depend largely for entertainment upon their intercourse with the ignorant, the coarse, and the poverty-stricken; that Fifth Avenue would die of ennui without the East Side. Is this true? Is it not true, on the contrary, that, socially speaking, like seeks like and that birds of a feather flock together, that comfort is offended by the sight of misery, that refinement is wounded by coarseness, and that the ideal of the intelligent is a society in which intelligence is universal?

Sixth. It is not proposed to realize the ideal of Nationalism by abrupt or revolutionary methods, but by the progressive nationalizing and municipalizing of existing public services and industries. It is proposed to begin by adding telegraph, telephone, and express services to the post office, according to the successful practice of foreign nations, by nationalizing the railroads and the coal-mining business, and by the municipalizing of all services now discharged for towns and cities by corporations. In all these measures three ends will be aimed at: First, to put an end to the present wholesale debauching of legislative bodies by the wealthy corporations now profiting by the services in question. Second, the increase of the cheapness and efficiency of those services which will result from conducting them for public use instead of private profit and from making them directly amenable as to shortcomings to popular criticism. Third, a radical improvement in the condition of the workers

126

in nationalized or municipalized business, including as features moderate hours of labor, safe and hygienic surroundings, with provision, proportioned at first to length of service, for sickness, accident, and age. The beginnings of a national productive and distributive system for the supply of public employees, at cost and not for profit, would follow. It is confidently believed that the nationalizing of a single important service, by experience of the benefits in all the aspects mentioned resulting from it, will by its effect upon public opinion greatly hasten the full adoption of the system.

Seventh. The nationalizing and municipalizing of the businesses mentioned, and of others, will not, as has been alleged, bring a body of voters under the political control of government. It is an essential principle of Nationalism that in all departments of public business only the chiefs and heads of departments are to be subject to executive appointment or removal. As to the main body of the force, it is proposed that each service shall be strictly graded, with admissions only to the lowest grade. Such admissions shall not be by appointment, but in skilled employments vacancies shall be filled by candidates in the order of their fitness as shown by prescribed tests of qualifications, and in the case of unskilled employments, not requiring special qualifications, by selection by lot from among applicants found generally qualified. Promotion is to be by record only, a matter of right and not of favor; removals to be only for cause, after a hearing before a board existing for the purpose, superiors having power to suspend subordinates pending inquiry. There is another sort of quite prevalent political intimidation to which, meanwhile, Nationalism will put an end so fast as it is applied to industry—that is, the intimidation of employees by private employers.

Eighth. Nationalism does not propose a paternal government, but its logical and practical antithesis, a co-operative administration for the benefit of equal partners. As a matter of propriety in the use of language, paternalism can only be ascribed to a government in proportion as it is non-popular, implying as the term does a relation of superiority and benevolence in the attitude of the government toward the people. Whatever errors of policy a popular government may fall into must be described by other terms than paternalism, inasmuch as their motives are not benevolence, but the supposed self-interest of the rulers themselves—that is, of the people. Nevertheless there does exist in this country today, despite our popular form of government, an unprecedented and most intolerable form of paternalism, against which Nationalism is a protest and a revolt. I refer to the capitalist and corporate paternalism resulting from the modern concentration of capital, whereby a few score individuals and corporations determine, arbitrarily and without regard to natural laws, on what terms the people of the United States shall eat, drink, and wherewithal they shall be clothed, what business they may do and what they may not, and whether they may do any at all, exercising by industrial and commercial methods a power in a hundred directions over the livelihood and concerns and very existence of the people, such as the most despotic government never dared assert, and which year by year and even

128

month by month is becoming more complete and inevitable.

This sort of paternalism, or, if I may coin the word, step-paternalism, Nationalism would make an end of. These stepfathers of the people Nationalists would depose. In irreconcilable opposition alike to governmental and to capitalist paternalism, Nationalists contend that the people have come of age, and should take their own business into their own hands.

Too much emphasis cannot be laid upon the fact that, setting wholly aside all moral, humane, Christian, industrial, and economical arguments for national co-operation, it has become a strictly political necessity, as the only way possible whereby to preserve republican equality and popular institutions against the vast aggregations of capital which are mastering the country. Any government, especially any popular government, which tolerates such mighty subjects, must end by becoming their tool. The conflict now upon us between plutocracy and the Republic is one compared with which the struggle between North and South was a superficial inflammation. The American people have overslept, but they are now awakening to the imminence and peril of the crisis. It is because Nationalism alone has proposed a plan whereby corporate power may be abolished while the advantages of concentrated capital are retained that it has met with popular acceptance. It is because the conditions of the problem admit of no other solution that its ultimate adoption may be safely predicted. If the Republic is to survive, not merely in name but in reality, it can only

129

be upon the industrial basis of national co-operation. Between plutocracy and Nationalism the election must finally be made. There is no third choice.

# Progress of Nationalism in the United States

## By Edward Bellamy

*(From the North American Review, June, 1892\*)*

TECHNICALLY, the term Nationalism as descriptive of a definite doctrine of social and industrial reform, was first used in 1888 by clubs made up of persons who sympathized with the ideas of a proper industrial organization set forth in "Looking Backward," and believed in the feasibility of their substantial adoption as the actual basis of society. Nationalism, in this strict sense, is the doctrine of those who hold that the principle of popular government by the equal voice of all, which, in advanced nations, is already recognized as the law of the political organization, should be extended to the economical organization as well; and that the entire capital and labor of nations should be nationalized, and administered by their people, through their chosen agents, for the equal benefits of all, under an equal law of industrial service.

In this sense of a definite philosophy and a positive programme, Nationalism is a plant of very recent growth. It would, however, be quite impossible to understand the reasons for its remarkable popularity and rapid

*Reprinted by special permission from The North American Review.

spread, and equally impossible to calculate the probabilities of its future development, without taking into account the evolutionary processes of which it is the outcome.

The very idea of the nation as an organization for the purpose of using the collective forces for the general protection and welfare, logically involved from the beginning, the extension of that organization to the industrial as well as to the political affairs of the people. Until the democratic idea became prevalent it was, however, possible for privileged classes to hold back this evolution; and so for unnumbered ages it has been held back. From the period at which the democratic idea gained ascendancy it could be a question of but a short time before the obvious interests of the majority of the people should lead to the democratizing of the national economic system to accord with the political system.

The Nationalist movement in the United States, instead of waiting till this late day, would have arisen fifty years ago as the natural sequence of the establishment of popular government and of the recognition that the national organization exists wholly and only for the promotion of the people's welfare, had it not been for the intervention of the slavery issue. It would indeed be more accurate to say that in a broad sense of the word the Nationalist movement did arise fifty years ago, for in spirit if not in form it may be said to date back to the forties. Those who are not familiar with the history of the extraordinary wave of socialistic enthusiasm which swept over the United States at that period and led to the Brook Farm Colony and a score of phalanster-

ies for communistic experiments, have missed one of the
most picturesque chapters of American history. Some
of the most eminent persons in the country, and many
who afterwards became eminent, were connected with
or in sympathy with these enterprises. That Horace
Greeley would very possibly have devoted himself to
some line of socialistic agitation, had not the slavery
struggle come on, will surely be questioned by none who
are familiar with his correspondence and early writings,
and in this respect he was representative of a large group
of strong and earnest spirits.

But slavery had to be done away with before talk of
a closer, kinder brotherhood of men was in order or, indeed, anything but a mockery. So it was that presently
these humane enthusiasts, these precursors of Nationalism, were drawn into the overmastering current of the
anti-slavery agitation. Then came the war, which should
be ranked the greatest in history, not merely on account
of the extent of the territory and of the vastness of the
armies involved, but far more because it issued, as such
a war never did before, in the speedy reconciliation of
the foes. The Reunion of the North and South after
the struggle is the best proof of the progress of humanity that history records, the best evidence that the Nationalist motto, "We war with systems not with men," is
not in advance of the moral sense of the nation we appeal
to.

The din of the fight had barely ceased when the progress of evolution towards economic Nationalism resumed
its flow with an impetus only heightened by its interruption. But social conditions meanwhile had profoundly

changed for the worse and with them the character of the economic controversy, which now became full of rancor and bitterness. The speculative opportunities offered by the war had developed the millionaire and his shadow, the tramp. Contrasts of wealth, luxury, and arrogance with poverty, want, and abjectness, never before witnessed in America, now on every side mocked the democratic ideal and made the republic a laughing-stock.

The panic of 1873, with the seven lean years that followed in its train, ushered in the epoch of acute industrial discontent in this country. Then began the war between labor and capital. The phenomena of the period have been, on the one hand, ever-enlarging aggregations of capital, and the appropriations of the business field by groups of great monopolies; and, on the other hand, unprecedented combinations of labor in trades-unions, federations of unions and the Knights of Labor. Both classes of phenomena, the combinations of capital and of labor, were equally significant of the evolution toward economic Nationalism. The rise of the Knights of Labor, the great trades-unions, the Federation of Trades, and on the agricultural side, of the Grangers, Patrons of Husbandry, Farmers' Alliances, and many other organizations, were demonstrating the feasibility of organizing the workers on a scale never dreamed of; while on the other side the enormous and ever-growing trusts and syndicates were proving the feasibility of organizing and centralizing the administration of capital on a scale of corresponding magnitude. Opposed as these two tendencies seemed, they were yet destined to be combined in the synthesis of Nationalism, and were necessary stages in its evolution. Both alike in all their phases were blind gropings towards completer union, confessions of a necessity of organizing forces for common ends, that could find their only logical result in Nationalism, when the nation should become at once employed and employer, and labor and capital be blended in indistinguishable union.

Nor were there lacking, in the epoch spoken of, very conscious and definite appeals, although partial and inadequate ones, to the national idea as the proper line along which adequate remedies were to be sought. The greenback movement in its argument that the oppressions and inadequacies of the monetary system could only be removed by taking the issue of money wholly out of the control or influence of private persons and vesting it directly in the nation, was a distinct anticipation of Nationalism. The same idea was very evident in the proposition to reject the gold or silver standard as the basis of money and rest it broadly on the nation's assets and the nation's credit. It is true, indeed, that Nationalism, by making the nation the only storekeeper, and its relations of distribution with each citizen a direct one, excluding middlemen, will dispense with buying and selling between individuals, and render greenbacks as superfluous as other sorts of money. Nevertheless, in the spirit of its appeal to the national idea, Greenbackism was strongly tinctured with the sentiment of Nationalism.

Another of the fragmentary anticipations of Nationalism during the period referred to was the rise of the Knights of Labor. The peculiar merit of this admirable body is the broadly humane basis of its organization, which gives it an ethical distinction necessarily lacking to the mere trades-union. Its motto, "An injury to one is the concern of all," if extended to all classes, would be a good enough one for the most thorough-going Nationalist. The Knights of Labor, like the Greenbackers, believed in the national idea and in dealing with the most formidable and dangerous class of private monopolies in this country, demanded the nationalization of the railroads.

In enumerating the streams of tendency which were during this period converging towards Nationalism, mention should also be made of the various anti-monopoly parties that from time to time arose as local and more or less national parties. The platforms of some of these parties were extremely radical, and the dominant idea in the suggestion of remedies was an appeal to the nation.

Finally came the Henry George agitation. The extraordinary impression which Mr. George's book, "Progress and Poverty," produced was a startling demonstration of the readiness of the public for some radical remedy of industrial evils. It is unnecessary to remind my readers that the nationalization of land was Mr. George's original proposition.

The foregoing considerations may perhaps sufficiently indicate how far back in American history the roots of Nationalism run, and how it may indeed be said to have been logically involved in the very principle of popular government on which the nation was founded.

A book of propaganda like "Looking Backward" produces an effect precisely in proportion as it is a bare anticipation in expression of what everybody was thinking and about to say. Indeed, the seeming paradox might almost be defended that in proportion as a book is effective it is unnecessary. The particular service of the book in question was to interpret the purport and direction of the conditions and forces which were tending towards Nationalism, and thereby to make the evolution henceforth a conscious, and not, as previously, an unconscious, one. The Nationalist who accepts that interpretation no longer sees in the unprecedented economical disturbances of the day a mere chaos of conflicting forces, but rather a stream of tendencies through ever larger experiments in concretation and combination towards the ultimate complete integration of the nation for economic as well as for political purposes. The sentiment of faith and good cheer born of this clear vision of the glorious end, and of the conviction that the seemingly contradictory and dangerous phenomena of the times are necessary means to that end, distinguishes the temper of the Nationalist as compared with that of other schools of reformers.

The first Nationalist Club was organized in Boston by readers of "Looking Backward" in 1888. Almost simultaneously other clubs were organized in all parts of the country, something like one hundred and fifty having been reported within the following two years, the reporting having, however, been very laxly attended to. There never was, perhaps, a reform movement that got along with less management than that of the Nationalists. There has never been any central organization and little

137

if any mutual organization of the clubs. Wherever in any community a few men and women have felt in sufficiently strong sympathy with the ideas of the Nationalists to desire to do something to spread them, they have formed an organization and gone ahead, with as much or little communication with other similar organizations as they have desired to have. While these clubs have been and are of the greatest use, and have accomplished remarkable results in leaving entire communities with Nationalism, there has never been any special effort to multiply them or otherwise to gather the whole body of believers into one band. We like to think that not one in a hundred who more or less fully sympathize with us, is a member of a Nationalist club or probably ever will be until the nation becomes the one Nationalist Club.

The practical work of the organized Nationalists for the past four years has, of course, been chiefly educational, consisting in the effort, by lectures, books, and periodicals, to get their ideas before the people. The lack of a central organization on the part of the clubs prevents, very fortunately, the existence of any formal "official" organ. The nearest approach to such a publication was at first the Nationalist, a monthly, issued in Boston, which a year and a half ago was succeeded by The New Nation, a weekly, edited by the present writer, and devoted to the exposition of the principles and purposes of Nationalism, with the news of the movement.

In the brief period that has elapsed since the origin of the Nationalist movement, with its clearly defined philosophy and positive purpose, the growth of Nationalism in this country has been accelerated in an extraordinary manner. While it is impossible not to ascribe the acceleration largely to the literature and work of the Nationalists, it is not for a moment intended to imply that this growth is solely attributable to the strictly Nationalist propaganda. Throughout this paper the argument has been maintained that this specific movement is but the outcome of forces long in operation, which, by no means as yet wholly coalescing with strict Nationalism, continue to work consciously or unconsciously towards the same inevitable result.

It is unnecessary surely, to do more than call attention to the great moral awakening upon the subject of social responsibilities and the ethical side, or rather the ethical soul and centre of the industrial question which has taken place within a very recent time. It was but yesterday that the pulpit was dumb on this class of themes, dumb because its hearers were deaf. Now, every Sunday hundreds of pulpits throughout the land are preaching social duty and the solidarity of nations and of humanity; declaring the duty of mutual love and service whereby the strong are made bondmen to the weak, to be the only key to the social problem. This is the very soul of Nationalism. To be able to present this theme effectively has become the best passport of the clergyman to popular success, the secret of full houses. One of the most hopeful features of the Nationalist outlook from the first has been the heartiness with which a large contingent of the clergy has enlisted in it, claiming that it was, as it truly is, nothing more than Christianity applied to industrial organization. This we hope to make so apparent that ere long all Christian men shall be obliged either to abjure Christ or come with us.

The recent change in the trend of economic discussion as to the questions involved in the proposition of Nationalism has not been less marked than the moral awakening. Until very recently this country was twenty-five years behind the intelligence and practice of Europe as to sociological questions. That there might be such awkward things as strikes we had indeed, learned since 1873; but that there was any such thing as a great industrial social question, of which these were but symptoms, had not dawned upon the public or on old-fashioned economists, who supposed that wisdom had died with Adam Smith. Remember that it was only a little while ago that "the social evil" was understood to refer exclusively to a special form of vice. It was imagined that there could not be any other social evil of consequence here in America unless, perhaps, it were intemperance in the use of alcoholic stimulants or tobacco. While the "effete monarchies of Europe" might have to rectify their institutions from time to time to keep pace with human progress, we rested in the serene conviction that General Washington and Mr. Jefferson had arranged our affairs for all time, and that Negro slavery was the last problem we should have to dispose of. And let it be observed that these great patriots in setting up popular self-government, did give us a finality of principle, but that an economic as well as a political method, in order to give effect to that principle, has now becomes necessary.

Where is now that easy complacency over the social

situation which so recently was the prevailing temper of our people? Economic discussion and the debate of radical social solutions absorb the attention of the country, and are the preponderating topics of serious conversations. Economic papers have the precedence in our periodicals, and, even in the purely literary magazine, they crowd the novel and the romance. Indeed, the novel with a sociological motive now sets the literary fashion and a course in political economy has become necessary to write a successful love story.

It is not so much the increased volume of economic discussion that marks the social growth of Nationalism, as the fact that its tone is chiefly given by the adherents of the new and humane schools of political economy which, until recently, had obtained but little hearing among us. Up to within a very few years the old school of political economy, although it had long before begun to fall into discredit in Europe, still held practically undisputed sway in America. Today the new school, with its socialistic method and sympathies, is the school to which nearly all the young and rising professors of political economy belong. The definition of labor as "a commodity," would now endanger the position of an instructor in that science in any institution of learning which did not depend for its patronage upon a reputation for being behind the times. There are a few such yet despite the growth of Nationalism.

The full programme of Nationalism, involving the entire substitution of public for private conduct of all business, for the equal benefit of all, is not indeed advocated by any considerable number of economists or prominent

141

writers. They discuss chiefly details of the general problem, but, in so far as they propose remedies, it is significant that they always take the form of state and national management of business. It would not probably be too strong a statement to say that the majority of the younger schools of political economists and economic writers on that subject, now regard with favor state conduct of what they call "natural monopolies," that is to say, telegraphs, telephones, railroads, local transit lines, waterworks, municipal lighting, etc. "Natural monopolies" are distinguished by this school as businesses in which the conditions practically exclude competition. Owing to the progress of the trusts and syndicates, businesses not natural monopolies are rapidly being made artificial ones with the effect of equally excluding competition. If the economists of the "natural monopoly" school follow the logic of their method they are bound, in proportion as the progress of artificial monopolization abolishes their distinction, to become full-fledged Nationalists. I have no doubt they will soon be wholly with us, as in spirit and tendency they now are.

There is a great deal more that might be said of the recent and swiftly increasing movement of moral sentiment and scientific thought towards Nationalism, but the limits of my space compel me to pass on to the consideration of what has been accomplished in the field of politics and legislation within the four years since its rise as a definitive doctrine.

The immediate propositions of the Nationalists are on two lines. First the nationalization of inter-State business, and business in the products or service of which people in more than one State are interested. Second, the State management or municipalization of businesses purely local in their relations. In the former line the rise within two years of a third national political party, pledged to a large part of the immediate purposes of Nationalism, is certainly the most notable phenomenon. The People's Party was formed at Cincinnati on February 22, 1891, and ratified and indorsed at St. Louis, May 19, 1892, by a convention representing the great Farmer's Alliances, white and colored, of the West and South, and also the Knights of Labor and other artisans' organizations. The platform adopted at St. Louis as that on which the People's Party's Presidential candidates are to be nominated and supported by these allied organizations, demands nationalization of the issue of money, nationalization of banking by means of postal savings-banks for deposit and exchange, national ownership and operation of the telegraphs and telephones, national ownership and operation of the railroads, and declares the land with its natural resources the heritage of the nation.

Remember that this platform voices the enthusiastic convictions and determination of many million voters belonging to organizations which have already carried several State elections, and which as now united may carry in the Presidential election, as their opponents concede, four or five states, and, as they themselves expect, twice or thrice that number. If you would estimate the probable growth of Nationalism in the next six months, remember that during that period the demands of this platform and the arguments for them will be stated and reiterated weekly by the eight to ten hundred farmers' papers of the South and West, and dinned into their ears by regiments of orators. About half the farmers' weeklies of the West, it should be added, not only support the St. Louis platform, but take every occasion to declare that the adoption of the whole Nationalist plan, with the industrial republic as its consummation, is but a question of time. "Talk about Nationalism," said one brawny farmer at the St. Louis convention, "why, west of the Mississippi we are all Nationalists."

In tracing the rise of this third party, it may be interesting to note that it was in the trans-Mississippi States, in the newly-admitted States and the Territories, and on the Pacific Coast, where the People's Party now has its main strongholds, that the reception of "Looking Backward" was most general and enthusiastic. The growing economic distress in the great grain States had no doubt much to do with this readiness for a radical industrial solution, but the bold adventurous temper of the people, perhaps, even more. To a race of pioneers which had hewn mighty States out of the wilderness and the desert within the lifetime of a generation, there was nothing to take the breath away in a proposal to reconstruct industry on new lines.

I have left myself little space wherein to speak of what has been done for Nationalism in the line of the municipalization of local businesses. The Nationalists of Boston and vicinity, in 1889 circulated petitions for the passage of a bill by the Legislature, permitting municipalities to build and operate their own lighting plants, gas or electric. The bill failed in the Legislature of 1889-90, passing the House but being lost in the Senate. The Nationalists resumed the fight the next year on petitions bearing 13,000 names. The bill became a law after a bitter fight, in which the Nationalists, backed by the labor organizations and a strong popular sentiment, were opposed by a combination of the electric and gas companies representing $35,000,000 of capital.

Prior to that date, public lighting, although long a matter of course in Great Britain and Europe, was almost unknown in America; a striking illustration, by the way, of the incomprehensible manner in which America has lagged behind monarchial and aristocratic states in the practical application of its own patented idea of popular government.

Up to the passage of the Municipal Lighting Bill in 1891 by the Massachusetts Legislature, less than a dozen American towns had tried public lighting, and few people had even heard of their experiment. In the one year since then sixteen towns and cities in Massachusetts alone and as many in Ohio, have taken steps toward public-lighting works, while a host of municipalities in the rest of the Union are following their example.

If the Nationalists had done nothing more than point out the way of deliverance from the gas-meter, they would surely have deserved well of the American people, but in doing that they have done more—they have set the people thinking along the line of municipal self-help.

The American citizen is not unintelligent as to questions of profit and loss. Give him the A B C of a business proposition and he can usually be trusted to go through the alphabet without further assistance. Once convince him that public light service means, as a matter of demonstration and experience, as it does, a saving to the consumer of from 30 to 50 per cent, and he will commence to scratch his head and ask why the same rule doesn't apply to water-works and transit systems.

By turning over such functions to private companies aiming only at the largest possible profits, instead of discharging them directly, cities and towns subject themselves to a needless tax, aggregating more, in many cases, than the total tax levy for nominally public purposes, as if, indeed, any purpose could be more public than lighting, water supply and transit. Wherever a private company can make a profit in serving the community (leaving aside watered stock) the people themselves, who take no profit from themselves, can do it just so much cheaper. All we Nationalists want to do is to get people to reason along the line of their collective interests with the same shrewdness they show in pursuing their personal interests. That habit once established, Nationalism is inevitable.

# Why Every Workingman Should Be a Nationalist

## By Edward Bellamy

*(From the Building Trades' Council Souvenir, April, 1893)*

NOTHING in the world is more certain than that every working man is bound to be a nationalist just as soon as he gets it fairly into his head what nationalism means, and what nationalists are trying to do. To put the whole thing in a sentence, what we are driving at is to extend popular government, the rule of the people, to industry and commerce. That is to say, we want to give the people the same voice in the regulation and direction of the industrial and commercial machine which they already have in regard to the political machine.

Look a moment at the contrast between the way our political government is regulated, and the way in which our industrial and commercial system is administered. Our political system is democratic, that is to say, it is governed by the people. Every man, be he dull or clever, rich or poor, has the same voice in it. It is in fact a popular government. On the other hand, our industrial and commercial system, the productive and distributing machinery of the country, is not controlled by the people, nor have they any voice in it. A small num-

147

ber of individuals and groups of individuals own and run it purely for their own profit, without any authority from the people, or any responsibility to the people, and with no reference whatever to anybody's interests but their own. So we have side by side, democracy in politics and despotism in industry and economics.

Now which is the more important to all of us who are not beyond the need of earning a living, to have a voice about the few and comparatively insignificant matters that belong to political administration, or to have a voice in governing the industrial system of production and distribution on which our livelihood depends  Can there possibly be two opinions about this? Is it not a sham and a lie to call a nation a republic, and a system democratic in which the people are allowed once in four years to decide which of two politicians shall draw a $50,000 salary as president, but denied any voice at all in regulating the system of production and distribution on which depends all that makes life worth living?

That is what we nationalists think and say, and what we want to do is to make this and every other nation a true republic, a real democracy, by bringing the entire business system of the country under the same popular government which now extends only to the few comparatively trifling functions called political.

Now you see exactly what we are aiming at in seeking to bring about the public operation of lighting plants, water-works, tramways, ferries, canals, telegraphs, telephones, railroads, express service, coal mines, and so on, indefinitely. These are all steps, small steps sometimes, but logical ones, toward the complete assertion of popular government over the entire field of production and distribution.

When this program is fulfilled there will be no private capitalists left to demand dividends or profits, and the proceeds of the national industries will be disposed of by the voice of the people, as the directors of the national corporation, and because the vote of all the directors will be equal it will follow that the dividend will have to be equal. That is to say the end of nationalism will be the economic or wealth equality of all citizens; all being on the other hand, required to render service according to their gifts and choice.

But are the weak and the women to share equally with the strong men? Most surely! It would never do to let the strong get the advantages of complete social co-operation while evading its duties. Even in the present imperfect system of society, this law of equal sharing in results, even though contributions are very unequal, is recognized in all the relations of the citizens to organized society. Taxes are paid in very unequal amounts, but are expended for the equal use of all. So military service in combines where it is universally required, is rendered very unequally by men and not at all by women; yet all alike are equally entitled to the full military protection of the nation in case of need.

If you do not care to look so far ahead as to the full triumph of nationalism, the immediate advantages of each step in its program are plain and large enough to command your support, quite apart from the ultimate result. The substitution of public for private control of any business means at once its great cheapening, for public oper-

149

ation is quite or nearly at cost. The public operation of a business, moreover, at once makes a public official of every employee in it, and everybody knows that public employment in a republican country, as compared with private employment, means respectful treatment, reasonable hours, the best rates of pay and comparative security of position. It means, in fact, a management responsible to public opinion, instead of the arbitrary rule of private capital aiming at profit only. Every business thus nationalized or municipalized is one more blow at the power which private capitalism exercises in the labor and goods markets and in legislative lobbies against the interests of the people at large, and working men in particular.

Organized capital is beating organized labor all along the line, but a vote for the public operation of monopolies is a club by which the working man can, and eventually will, defeat and overthrow organized capital, and it is the only weapon by which that end can be accomplished.

As we said at the outset, nothing in the world is more certain than that every workingman is bound to become a nationalist as soon as he clearly understands what nationalism is.

# The Programme of the Nationalists

## By Edward Bellamy

*(From The Forum, March, 1894\*)*

I HAVE been asked to give some account of Nationalism with a statement of its programme and of the first
steps to be taken in the logical development of the plan,
with especial reference to America, though it is of course
to be observed that the economic situation in the United
States differs from that in older nations only in the suddenness with which oppressive conditions have been developed which in Europe are of ancient standing.

Nationalism is economic democracy. It proposes to
deliver society from the rule of the rich, and to establish
economic equality by the application of the democratic
formula to the production and distribution of wealth. It
aims to put an end to the present irresponsible control
of the economic interests of the country by capitalists
pursuing their private ends, and to replace it by responsible public agencies acting for the general welfare. That
is to say, it is proposed to harmonize the industrial and
commercial system with the political, by bringing the former under popular government, as the latter has already
been brought, to be administered as the political government is, by the equal voice of all for the equal benefit of
all. As political democracy seeks to guarantee men

---

\*Reprinted by special permission from The Forum Magazine.

against oppression exercised upon them by political forms, so the economic democracy of Nationalism would guarantee them against the much more numerous and grievous oppressions exercised by economic methods. The economic democracy of Nationalism is indeed the corollary and necessary supplement of political democracy, without which the latter must forever fail to secure to a people the equalities and liberties which it promises.

The conditions which justify the present Nationalist agitation, especially in America, may be broadly stated in brief terms.

It is certainly self-evident that the manner of the organization and administration of the economic system which regulates the production and distribution of wealth, whereupon not only the entire welfare but even the bare lives of all depend, is infinitely more important to a people than the manner in which any other part of their affairs is regulated. The economic system of the United States was formerly, and within the memory of men now living, one which offered a fairly free field to individual enterprise, with some opportunity for all to acquire a comfortable livelihood if not wealth; and in consequence of this fact, despite many inequalities of condition a good degree of popular contentment has until recent times prevailed.

By an economic revolution unprecedented in scope and rapidity of movement, these former conditions have been within the time of one generation, and chiefly within twenty years, completely transformed. In place of a field of free competition with a fair opportunity for indi-

152

vidual initiative in every direction, our economic system now presents the aspect of a centralized government, or group of governments, administered by great capitalists and combinations of capitalists, who monopolize alike the direction and the profits of the industries of the people.

Although the economic rulers who have thus crushed out individual enterprise in this country control interests incomparably more important to the people than are the functions exercised by the so-called political government, yet, while our political governors hold power only by delegation from the people, and are strictly accountable to them for its exercise, those rulers who administer the economic government of the country, and hold the livelihood of the people in their hands, are not elected or in any way delegated to do so by the people, and admit no accountability to them for the manner in which they exercise their power.

Scorning the decent hypocrisies by which other sovereigns have been wont to cloak their pretensions, the capitalists who have mastered our economic government do not justify their rule by pretending either the divine right of kings, the consent of the governed, or even a benevolent intention toward their subjects. They claim no other title to power than their ability to suppress resistance, and expressly avow personal gain as the sole motive of their policy. In pursuance of this end the administration of the economic government of the country has been so conducted as to concentrate in the hands of an insignificant proportion of the people the bulk of the wealth which must furnish the general means of subsistence.

Fifty years ago, when, with the application of steam to machinery, the power of capital relatively to labor was suddenly multiplied, this country was held to be the ideal democracy of history on account of the prevailing equality in the distribution of wealth, and the general contentment and public spirit on the part of the people consequent thereon. At the present time 31,000 men are reputed to possess one-half of the wealth upon which 65,000,000 persons depend for existence, and the greater part of the other half is owned by a small additional fraction of the population, leaving the vast numerical majority of the nation without any considerable stake in the country. By the latest estimates, based upon the returns of the census of 1890, 9 per cent of the population of the United States owns 71 per cent of the wealth of the country, leaving but 29 per cent to the remaining 91 per cent of the population; and 4,074 persons or families, being the richest group among the 9 per cent mentioned, own one-fifth of the total wealth of the country, or nearly as much as the aggregate holdings of 91 per cent of the people.

History records no expropriation of a nation so complete as this, effected within so short a time, since the ages when military conquest meant the wholesale confiscation of the goods and persons of the conquered people. The population of Europe, indeed, groan under similar conditions, but with them they are the heritage of past ages, not, as in America the result of an economic revolution effected within one lifetime.

# THE PROGRAMME OF THE NATIONALISTS

This drainage of the nation's wealth to enrich a petty class has produced extraordinary social changes and portends more disastrous ones. Our farming population, constituting the bulk of the people, and in the past the most prosperous and contented portion, the main support of the republic in peace and war, has been converted by intolerable economic pressure, and the prospect of being reduced to the condition of a peasantry, into the most revolutionary class in the nation. The transformation in the conditions of the artisans has not been less disastrous. With the consolidation of capital in vast masses under corporate management, all that was humane in the relation of employer and employed has disappeared, and mutual suspicion and hatred and an attitude of organized hostility have taken their place. It has become the chief function of the militia to overawe strikers and suppress the disturbances of discontented working men. We are being taught by object-lessons of startling frequency that our industrial system, like the political systems of Europe, rests, in the end, upon the bayonet. The old-world caste distinctions of upper, lower, and middle classes—terms abhorrent to our fathers—are being rapidly adopted among us, and mark only too justly the disintegration of our once integral and coherent communities into mutually embittered elements which the iron bands of political despotism will soon be needed to hold together in a State.

In view of this situation, which has resulted from the conquest and exploitation of our economic system by an irresponsible and despotic oligarchy, Nationalists maintain that if the people of the United States would retain

155

any part of the high estate of equality, liberty, and material welfare which formerly made them the world's envy, it is full time for them, in the exercise of their supreme power over governments and institutions, to make an end of the usurpation which has so imperiled their condition, and to establish in its place a new system of economic administration, "laying its foundations in such principles, and organizing its powers in such form, as shall to them seem most likely to effect their safety and happiness."

What sort of an industrial and economic government shall the people establish in place of the present irresponsible rule of the rich? The question answers itself to a certain extent; for, if the people establish the government, manifestly it must be a popular government. But another question remains. Shall this government be exercised by the people individually, or collectively? Shall we seek to restore the state of things which existed half a century and more ago, when independent individual enterprise was the rule in every field of industry and commerce, and a hundred competitive concerns did the business now attended to by one? Even if it were desirable to bring back that era, it would be as much out of the question as to restore the virgin continent, the boundless resources, the unoccupied lands, and the other material conditions that made it possible.

The industrial system that is to employ and maintain our dense population, under the present and future conditions of the country, must be a systematized, centralized, interlocking economic organization of the highest efficiency. It is a physical impossibility to restore to the people, as individuals, the government of their economic interests; but it is feasible to bring it under their collective control, and that is the only possible alternative to economic oligarchy or, as it is called, plutocracy. This is the programme of Nationalism. We hold that the industrial system of a nation, like its political system, ought to be a government of the people, by the people, for the people, and for all of them equally. To that end we desire to see organized as public business all the industrial and commercial affairs of the people, so that they may be carried on henceforth, like all other public business, by responsible public agents, for the equal benefit of all citizens.

This plan is called Nationalism because it proceeds by the nationalization of industries, including, as minor applications of the same principle, the municipalization and State control of localized businesses.

Socialism implies the socializing of industry. This may or may not be based upon the national organism, and may or may not imply economic equality. As compared with socialism, Nationalism is a definition not in the sense of apposition or exclusion, but of a precision rendered necessary by a cloud of vague and disputed implications historically attached to the former word.

Perhaps the most common objection to the plan of nationalizing industry and carrying it on as public business is that it will involve more government. It is not so. Nationalization will simply substitute one sort of government for another. The industrial system which has grown up in the United States is, as we have shown, a government of the most rigid and despotic sort. In place of the irresponsible masters who now rule the economic interests of the people with a rod of iron, Nationalism will substitute popular self-government. Thomas Jefferson is quoted as saying that the government that governs least is self-government. That was what the signers of the American Declaration of Independence thought when they insisted on setting up a government of their own in spite of King George's willingness to manage their affairs for them. That is what Nationalists think in advocating popular government of the people's industrial interests in place of the present economic oligarchy.

It will tend to a clear understanding of the programme of Nationalism if we distinguish carefully between the features of the plan considered as fully carried out, and as in process of introduction. Many of the most certain and necessary consequences of Nationalism when fully carried out, must remain till then quite impracticable. Among these is the principle of the indefeasible economic equality of all citizens, without regard, of course, to sex.

Economic equality is the obvious corollary of political equality as soon as the economic system is democratized. Quite apart from ethical considerations in its favor, it follows, as a matter of course, from the equal voice of all in determining the method of distribution. Whatever a democratic State undertakes must be undertaken for the common—that is the equal—benefit of all. The European socialists, or a large part of them, do not insist upon economic equality, but allow economic variations in the ideal State. This is because they do not, like the Nationalists, deduce their conclusions by the rigid application of the democratic idea to the economic system.

# THE PROGRAMME OF THE NATIONALISTS

But while economic equality is the Keystone of National-ism, it must wait till the nation has fully organized its productive system. The arch must be finished before the keystone is placed, though after it is placed the stability of the arch depends upon it.

While Nationalists recognize as legitimate the demand for something definite in the way of a programme from a party of radical reform, it is not to be inferred that they pretend to forecast with exactness the course of events. Great revolutions, however peaceful they may be, do not follow prearranged plans, but make channels for themselves of which we may at best predict the general direction and outcome. Meanwhile Nationalists would prepare the way by a step-by-step extension of the public conduct of business, which shall go as fast or as slow as public opinion may determine.

In making any industry or service public business, two ends should be kept equally in view, viz.: first, the bene-fit of the public by more cheap, efficient, and honest service or commodities; and second, but as an end in every way equally important, the immediate ameliora-tion of the condition of workers taken over from private into public service. As to the first point, whenever a service or business is taken over to be publicly conducted, it should be managed strictly at cost; that is to say, the service or product should be furnished at the lowest cost that will pay the expense and proper charges of the busi-ness. Nationalism contemplates making all production for use and not for profit, and every nationalized busi-ness should be a step in that direction by eliminating profit so far as it is concerned.

159

# EDWARD BELLAMY SPEAKS AGAIN!

As to the improvement in the condition of the workers, which is the other and equal end to be sought in all cases of nationalizing a business, it is enough to say that the State should show itself the model employer. Moderate hours of labor, healthful and safe conditions, with provision for sickness, accident, and old age, and a system for the admission, promotion, and discharge of employees strictly based on merit, and absolutely exclusive of all capricious personal interference for political or other reasons, should characterize all publicly conducted business from the start. In particular cases, such as the clothing manufacture now so largely carried on by sweaters' slaves, decent wages and conditions might temporarily raise the price of ready-made clothing. If it did it would only show how necessary it had been to make the business a State monopoly; and we may add that, on grounds of humanity, this is one of the first that should be brought under public management.

As to the general question as to the order in which different branches of business should be nationalized, or (which is the same thing) brought under municipal or State control, ownership, and operation, Nationalists generally agree that chartered businesses of all sorts, which, as holding public franchises, are already quasi-public services, should first receive attention. Under this head come telegraphs and telephones, railroads both local and general, municipal lighting, water-works, ferries and the like. The railroads alone employ some 800,000 men, and the employees in the other businesses mentioned may raise that figure to 1,000,000, representing perhaps a total population of 4,000,000, certainly a rather big slice of the nation to begin with. These businesses would carry with them others. For example, the railroads are the largest consumers of iron and steel, and national operation of them would naturally carry with it the national operation of the larger part of the iron business. There are about 500,000 iron-workers in the country, implying a population of perhaps 2,000,000 dependent on the industry, and making with the railroad and other employees and their dependents, some 6,000,000 persons. The same logic would apply to the mining of coal, with which, as carrier and chief consumer, the railroads are as closely identified.

The necessity of preserving what is left of our forests will soon force all the States to go into the forestry business, which may well be the beginning of public operation of the lumber industry. If our fast-vanishing fisheries are to be protected, not merely national supervision, but national operation, will soon be necessary.

In the field of general business, the trusts and syndicates which have so largely stimulated the popular demand for Nationalism have also greatly simplified its progress. Whenever the managers of any department of industry or commerce have, in defiance of law and public interest, formed a monopoly, what is more just and proper than that the people themselves, through their agents, should take up and conduct the business in question at cost? In view of the fact that most of the leading branches of production have now been "syndicated," it will be seen that this suggestion, fully carried out, would go far toward completing the plan of Nationalization.

Meanwhile the same process would be going on upon other lines. Foreign governments which have large armies, in order to secure quality and cheapness, usually manufacture their soldiers' clothing, rations, and various supplies in government factories. The British government, which is most like our own, was forced by the swindling of contractors to go into making clothing for the soldiers in the Crimean War, and has since kept it up with most admirable results. If our government had manufactured the soldiers' supplies in the Civil War, it would have saved a vast sum of money. It is highly desirable that it should forthwith begin to manufacture clothing and other necessaries for its soldiers and sailors, and for any other of its employees who might choose to be so served, as it is safe to say all would; for goods as represented, proof against adulteration, and furnished at cost, would be a godsend even to a millionaire in these days of knavish trade. This policy of supplying the needs of government employees with the product of publicly conducted industries would bring about the whole productive and distributive plan of Nationalism in proportion as the number of employees increased.

Among special lines of business which ought at once to be brought under public management are the liquor traffic and fire and life insurance. It is proposed that every State should immediately monopolize the liquor traffic within its borders, and open places of sale in such localities as desire them. The liquors should be sold at cost —that is to say, at rates to pay all expenses of the system, —by State agents, whose compensation should be fixed without relation, direct or indirect, to the amount of sales.

162

# THE PROGRAMME OF THE NATIONALISTS

This plan would eliminate desire of profit as a motive to stimulate sales, would ensure a strict regard to all conditions and requirements of law, and would guarantee pure liquors. Pending the nationalization of the manufacture of liquors, the general government need be called on only for a transportation law protecting the States against illegal deliveries within their borders.

As to State life and fire insurance, this undertaking would need no plant and no backing save the State's credit on long-tested calculations of risks. It would be done at cost, in State buildings, by low-salaried officials, and without any sort of competitive or advertising expenses. This would mean a saving to fire insurers of at least 25 per cent in premiums, and of at least 50 per cent to life insurers, and would, above all, give insurance that was not itself in need of being re-insured.

When private plants are taken over by a city, state, or nation, they should of course be paid for; the basis of valuation being the present cost of a plant of equal utility. Of course this subject of compensation should be considered in view of the fact that the ultimate effect of Nationalism will be the extinction of all economic superiorities, however derived.

The organization of the unemployed on a basis of State-supervised co-operation is an urgent undertaking in line with the programme of Nationalism. The unemployed represent a labor force which only lacks organization to be abundantly self-sustaining. It is the duty and interest of the State to so organize the unemployed, according to their several trades and aptitudes,—the women workers as well as the men,—that their support shall be provided for out of their own product, which should not go upon the market for sale, but be wholly consumed within the circle of the producers, thus in no way deranging outside prices or wages. This plan contemplates the unemployed problem as being a permanent one, with periods of special aggravation, and as therefore demanding for its solution a permanent and elastic provision for a circle of production and consumption complete in itself and independent of the commercial system. There is no other method for dealing with the unemployed problem which does not mock it.

In proportion as the industries, commerce, and general business of the country are publicly organized, the source of the power and means of the growth of the plutocracy, which depend upon the control and revenues of industry, will be undermined and cut off. In the same measure, obviously, the regulation of the employment of the people and the means of providing for their maintenance will pass under their collective control. To complete the plan of Nationalism by carrying out its guarantee of equal maintenance to all with employment according to fitness, will require only a process of systematization and equalizing of conditions under an already unified administration.

The work of Nationalists has hitherto been chiefly educational. This must necessarily have been the case from the magnitude of the scheme, requiring, as it does, something like national acceptance for the undertaking of its larger features. In the department, especially, of local public services, such as waterworks, lighting, transit, and the like, something like a wave of feeling in favor of the municipalization of such undertakings has within three years swept over the country, and, far from subsiding, is swelling into a tide. In nearly every progressive community there has sprung up within a few years a more or less strong nucleus of citizens which meets every fresh oppression of chartered corporations with the demand for public operation. The insolent taunt of intrenched monopoly—"What are you going to do about it?"—no longer strikes the people dumb. An answer is on every lip, and it is,—Nationalism! The sudden recent advance to the first rank among the topics of the day, in the news and periodical press, of the questions of the public operation of commerce and business as a remedy for capitalistic abuse, is of course the best general evidence of the extent to which the public mind is occupied with this subject.

Doubtless, however, the most startling single demonstration of the rapidity and solidity of the growth of Nationalism is the fact that in the Presidential campaign of 1892 more than one million votes were polled for the People's Party, the platform of which embodied the most important features of the immediate Nationalist programme as above stated. That even this platform was not radical enough to satisfy a large portion of the party and its sympathizers, has been made evident by the far more advanced ground taken subsequently by State and local conventions, by the great labor organizations in their national and local assemblies, and by the Farmer's Alliances. Indeed, the statement may be safely made, that, so far as the economic and industrial discontent in this country has hitherto found definite expres-

165

sion, it has taken the form of demands for the more or less complete application of the nationalization idea to business. This is simply because there is found to be, upon examination, no other way out.

Persons whose minds are first directed to Nationalism often miss the point by failing to see that it is inevitable, as the only alternative of plutocracy, if the latter is not to triumph. Such persons are wont to regard the nationalization or public conduct of industry as merely one economic device among many, to be compared with the rest as more or less attractive or ingenious. They fail to perceive that it is the necessary and only method by which a solution of the economic question can be secured which shall be democratic in character. Many who sincerely believe—or think they do—in popular government and the democratic idea as a general principle, would doubtless see this question differently, if they took time to consider that by the very meaning of the terms the public management of industry is the substitution of popular for class and personal government, and that in opposing it they stand squarely against the democratic idea and in favor of oligarchical rule in the most extensive and important department of human interests.

There are two principles on which the blended affairs of human beings in society may be regulated: Government by all for all, and Government by a few for a few. The time is at hand when it is to be determined whether the one principle or the other shall henceforth regulate the organization of human labor and the distribution of its fruits. The countless past combats in the immemorial struggle of the many against the few, whether for personal, religious, or political liberty, have but cleared the way and led up to this all-embracing, all-concluding issue, now being joined the world over. It is the decisive battle to which all the former engagements were but preliminary skirmishes.

Not in many ages, surely,—perhaps never,—have men and women, during their brief probations on earth, had an opportunity to make so momentous a mistake as those will who take the wrong side in this battle.

# Our Prospective Sovereigns

## By Edward Bellamy

*(From The Nationalist, July, 1889)*

FIRST of all, we must heed the cry of the children. We must deliver them from the taskmasters and turn them over to the schoolmasters. The present school system of Massachusetts with its wretched twenty weeks of compulsory attendance up to the age of fourteen, with grammar and high schools for a few fortunate ones, is not a serious attempt to educate the people, and it is time that this was said plainly. The age of fourteen is no time to bring to a close the education of a prospective sovereign of the United States and custodian of its liberties. Merely to raise the age limit of compulsory schooling to fifteen, sixteen, seventeen or eighteen would, however, not help matters, for the reason that, in the majority of instances, those parents who take their children out of school as soon as the law is off, do so because they must do so, because they are themselves too poor to support them longer in idleness. Now, whatever others may think, Nationalists do not consider that the inability, or even the thriftlessness of a parent, is any sufficient reason why a child should be condemned to the lifelong serfdom of ignorance. The duty the parent cannot or will not do toward his child the State must do.

169

## EDWARD BELLAMY SPEAKS AGAIN!

It is my earnest hope that the Nationalist clubs may see their way clear to formulating and presenting to the voters of the State as a test for legislative candidates at the next State election a demand for a law raising the age of compulsory education to at least seventeen years, and the school year to at least thirty-five weeks, with a sufficient State provision for the support of the children of indigent parents while at school. It appears to me that this is a measure which all persons who hope for the evolution of a better social order will be prepared to support. The children are of no party; the children have no enemies; and surely it is most rational to begin the reform of society with that portion of it which is most plastic, that is, with the children. The advocates of all modes and schools of reform must here agree, for under whatever figure we may severally fancy the hoped-for new order, we must depend upon the children, who now ought to be in school, to put it into effect. Those on the contrary, who disbelieve in all reform or progress, and hold that the present heart-rending social conditions are to endure forever, will be quite consistent in opposing the proposed measure. If their view is correct, the schools should all be closed and education forbidden the masses entirely, that, being more nearly brutalized, they may be less sensible of their degradation.

The attitude of persons on all important questions of improving the education of the masses will, I think, be found to correspond quite closely with their general belief on the larger question of the possibilities of human progress. One other point I want to speak of. The transfer to the schools of all children under seventeen now at work in stores, shops and factories would create a demand for adult labor which would not a little relieve the present glutted labor market. To make work by waste is poor political economy, but this would be to make work by saving—by saving the children.

# Looking Forward

## By Edward Bellamy

*(From The Nationalist, December, 1889)*

I T IS an indication of the ripeness of the times for the National plan of industry that the predominating economic facts and tendencies of the epoch so lend themselves to its aims as to leave no question as to the practical policy of the movement. In order to realize in due time the Nationalist idea it is only necessary to take judicious advantage of the contemporary tendency toward the consolidation of capital and concentration of business control. The "Ship of State" is already being borne onward by a current which it is only needful to utilize in order to reach the desired haven. The progressive nationalization and municipalization of industries by substituting public control for the public advantage, in place of already highly centralized forms of corporate control for corporate advantage, is at once the logical and the inevitable policy of Nationalism.

In looking forward, however, to the future of the movement, and forecasting the work it may be able to accomplish, it is impossible not to recognize that more after all will depend upon its spirit than its method. Its method scarcely can be other than the one indicated, and this is so obviously the natural, and not an arbitrary method, as to give the best of ground for confidence that

173

it is the right one. But an excellent method may be defeated by a bad spirit, while on the other hand, if the spirit be good and true, mistakes of method may be remedied, and will not prevent ultimate triumph. In offering some suggestions as to the spirit which should animate the Nationalist movement I do but describe what seems to me the characteristics of its present spirit and of the men and women engaged in it.

The first of these characteristics is unselfishness.

The sentiment of human brotherhood which is the animating principle of Nationalism is a religion in itself, and to understand it in its full significance implies a sense of consecration on the part of those who devote themselves to it. Nationalism, is indeed, based also upon the soundest of economic laws; the principle of fraternal cooperation is as certainly the only true science of wealth-production, as it is the only moral basis for society; but the latter is so much more the important consideration that even if a brotherly relation with our fellow-men could only be attained by the sacrifice of wealth, not the less would the true Nationalist seek it. The ultimate triumph of Nationalism demands as its first condition that it be kept upon the high moral ground it now occupies, and retain as its chief motive that pure and uncompromising enthusiasm of humanity which now animates it.

The second of the characteristics essential to the spirit of Nationalism, if it is to succeed speedily, is a tolerant and charitable attitude toward the critical and the indifferent—toward our opponents.

There is the more need of dwelling on this point as

there seems to be, curiously enough, something in the advocacy of reforms which tends to develop an intolerant and uncharitable spirit toward those who are not yet believers. And yet what could be more exquisitely absurd in itself than that spirit, on the part of a reformer, or more calculated to defeat his own supposed end. If it be true, as the tone of some reformers toward the rest of the world seems to indicate, that they are hopelessly better than the general mass of men, what expectation can they have of the success of their reform, since it can only succeed by converting these bad people? Until we call a man names, there is always a chance that we may convert him but, afterwards, none at all. And not only that, but we are not helping our case with the by-standers. It would seem plain that only reformers who have all the converts they need can afford to call their opponents names. There is especially one form of denunciation which Nationalists have thus far left to other sorts of social reformers, and it is hoped we may continue to. This is the denunciation of the wealthy in the supposed interests of the poor. Nothing could be more unjust and senseless. The rich could not, however disposed, abolish or greatly lessen poverty so long as the present industrial system remains. It is the system that is to be attacked and not individuals whose condition, whether of riches or poverty, merely illustrates its results. Of course, there are many rich men who have become so by vicious methods and these merit personal condemnation, but there are probably more to whose enterprise and leadership the community owes much of the little wealth and comfort it has. It is a very barbarous and wasteful sort of leadership, to be sure, and one for which we hope to substitute a mode of organizing industry infinitely more humane and efficient. But meanwhile let us not fall into the mistake of those who rant against capitalists in general, as if, pending the introduction of a better system, they were not,—no doubt selfishly, but yet in fact—performing a necessary function to keep the present system going.

It is the distinguishing quality of Nationalism and one on which its near success largely depends that it places the whole subject of industrial and social reform upon a broad National basis, viewing it not from the position or with the prejudices of any one group of men, but from the ground of a common citizenship, humanity and morality. Nationalism is not a class movement; it is a citizens' movement. It represents peculiarly neither men nor women, North nor South, black nor white, poor nor rich, educated nor ignorant, employers nor employed, but all equally; holding that all of us alike, whatever our label may be, are victims in body, mind or soul, in one way or another, of the present barbarous industrial and social arrangements, and that we are all equally interested, if not for our physical, yet for our moral advantage, if not for ourselves, yet for our children, in breaking the meshes which entangle us and struggling upward to a higher, nobler, happier plane of existence.

The third of the characteristics essential to the spirit of Nationalism is patriotism.

There are social reformers who believe, the less one's devotion to his own country and countrymen, the better he will love other countries and humanity at large, as if a man were usually found to be a better neighbor in proportion as he neglects his own family. This is a belief which Nationalists utterly repudiate. The very word Nationalism is an appeal to love of country. Patriotism, though so often misdirected, is the grandest and most potent form under which the enthusiasm of humanity has yet shown itself capable of moving great masses, and in its spirit is contained the promise and potency of the world-embracing love in which it shall some day merge. Social reforms must follow National lines and will succeed as they are able to adapt themselves to National conditions and sentiments and identify themselves with National traditions and aspirations. We as Americans do not, I am sure, love mankind any the less for the aspiration we cherish that, in the present world-wide movement for a better social order, America may maintain and justify that leadership of the nations which she assumed a century ago.

The fourth characteristic of the Nationalist movement which it must retain as a condition of success is its present spirit of conservatism as to methods, combined with uncompromising fidelity to ends.

Evolution, not revolution, orderly and progressive development, not precipitate and hazardous experiment, is our true policy. The intoxication of a mighty hope should not tempt us to forget that the success of the great reform to which we have set our hands depends not so much upon winning the applause of fellow-enthusiasts, welcome as this may be, as upon gaining and keeping the confidence of the law-abiding masses of the American people. To this end we have need to be careful that no party or policy of disorder or riot finds any countenance from us.   It is my own belief that on account of its peculiar adaptation to present economic and social states and tendencies Nationalism is destined to move rapidly, but it is for this very reason that prudence and conservatism are called for on the part of those identified with it.   Our mistakes alone can hinder our cause.

178

# "Looking Backward" Again

## By Edward Bellamy

*(From the North American Review, March, 1890\*)*

I DON'T mind admitting that I have greatly enjoyed the pleasant things which have been said about "Looking Backward," and am much obliged to those who have found it consistent with their consciences to say them. At the same time, I have read such serious criticisms of the book and its plan of industrial reform as have come to my notice with greater interest, if not greater pleasure, than the congratulatory notices. While holding it absolutely beyond question that the next phase of industry and society as based upon it, will be a plan of national cooperation, and that this plan cannot be permanently based upon any other principle than universal industrial service with equality of material condition, I recognize that the details of such a cooperative organization may be greatly varied consistently with these principles.

Though I advance in "Looking Backward" a series of details of such an organization, which seem to me not unreasonable, I have been far from considering them as necessarily the best devices possible, and have accordingly been on the lookout for valuable criticisms and sug-

---

\*Reprinted by special permission from The North American Review.

179

gestions. Perhaps this statement may be taken as a sufficient response to the large class of criticisms of "Looking Backward," which have addressed themselves to minor details of the manner of life depicted in the book. These, and even many more important points, may be safely left to the future to settle. The thing for us to settle—the only question which "Looking Backward" has raised which it is worth the time of serious men to discuss—is whether or not there has come to be, between the intellect and the conscience of men and the actual conditions of society and industry, such a degree of incongruity and opposition as to threaten the permanence of the existing order, and whether there is enough ground for faith in God and man to justify a hope that the present order may be replaced by one distinctly nobler and more humane.

The main objection which I make to the article by General Walker in the February "Atlantic," entitled 'Mr. Bellamy and the New Nationalist Party,' is that it totally fails to take into consideration this larger and only really important aspect of the subject. One is tempted to ask where General Walker has lived, that he is able to discuss "Looking Backward" and Nationalism wholly without reference to the present unprecedented ferment in the minds of men, which alone has given the book its circulation and the movement its impetus. Does he not know that thirty years ago "Looking Backward" would have fallen flat, and that the reason it has not done so today is that within this period a great revolution has taken place in the minds of reading men and women as to the necessity and possibility of radical social reform?

## "LOOKING BACKWARD" AGAIN

A criticism of "Looking Backward" in the January number of the "Contemporary Review," by the eminent French economist, Emile de Laveleye, deals with the subject in a manner so strongly contrasting with General Walker's superficial and often flippant tone that perhaps I cannot better indicate my meaning than by a quotation from the closing paragraph. M. Laveleye says:

"The rapid and extraordinary success in the Anglo-Saxon world of Mr. Bellamy's book is a symptom well worthy of attention. It proves that the optimism of the old-fashioned economists has entirely lost the authority that it formerly possessed. It is now no longer believed that in virtue of the laissez-faire principle everything will arrange itself for the best, in the best of all possible worlds. People feel that there is in very truth a *social question;* that is to say, that the division of the good things of this world is not in accordance with the laws of justice, and that something ought to be done to increase the share of the principal agents of production, the workmen."

M. Laveleye then quotes Dupont White:

"It was hoped that the (great modern) increase in the production of riches would secure satisfaction to all, but nothing of the sort has taken place. Discontent is greater and more deeply rooted than ever. From this deceived hope has been formed a new science. It may be called a social science, or it may even be said that it is not a science at all, but it is quite certain that charity in laws is a notion which in our day should be a fundamental doctrine, for beyond the pale of all sects of socialists it has sown in all hearts a feeling of uneasiness, of anxiety and care, an unknown emotion respecting the suffering classes, which has become a matter of public conscience."

While I must claim that the apparent lack on General

181

Walker's part of any such "feeling of uneasiness, of anxiety, and care," or any emotion whatever respecting the suffering classes, or any large view of the subject he discusses, distinctly disables him as a serious critic of Nationalism, I shall endeavor, to the best of my ability, to answer such specific criticisms as he has made.

The objection to the industrial organization outlined in "Looking Backward" to which General Walker devotes most space is its alleged excessively military character. From the stress he lays upon this point, it is evident that he has been seriously misled by the use of the term "army of industry," and by the analogy with the principle of universal military service which was used to illustrate the basis of industrial duty. He apparently labors under the impression that the rigid forms of military discipline are to be applied to the industrial force. It is evident that he has visions of the drill-ground, of the barracks, of the guard-house, and, for all I know, of drum-head courts-martial and firing squads. He protests against the nightmare which he himself has conjured up, in the following terms:

"Doubtless the industrial forces require to be organized and administered both firmly and judiciously, but it is not necessary that discipline shall be carried so far as to deprive the individual of his initiative, to take from him all freedom of choice, and to subject him to an authority which shall have over him the power of life and death, of honor and disgrace."

Now, these words precisely express my own convictions on the subject. I firmly believe, with General Walker, that while "industrial forces require to be organized and administered both firmly and judiciously," a harsh or

182

oppressive discipline is not necessary. What, then, is General Walker talking about, and whom is he talking at? If he thinks he is talking about the national army of industry, and its mode of organization and administration as contemplated by the author of "Looking Backward," or by the Nationalists, he is totally mistaken. While men who can work and will not work will doubtless be made to work, it is not believed that any more arduous discipline (or different conditions of life in any respect) will need to be imposed upon industrious men than the workers in any large and thoroughly systematized business at present undergo.

An ounce of fact is worth a pound of theory. There are several thousand clerks employed in the government departments at Washington on terms very similar to those which will obtain in the coming industrial army. The next time General Walker is in Washington it would be a good idea for him to step into one of the departments, and have a little chat with the clerks as to the amount of military discipline they are subjected to. There are some one or two hundred thousand post-office employees in the country. Has General Walker heard any rumors of a proposed wholesale desertion on their part by reason of the severity of their discipline? Does he understand—to use one of his own expressions as to the industrial army—that "they are obliged to surrender will, power of choice, freedom of movement, almost individuality"? If not, will he tell us why they should have to do so when their number shall be multiplied a hundred-fold?

Just here let me say in passing that the slight precau-

183

tion of looking about them, before going into convulsions over the plans of the Nationalists, would generally reveal to our critics the working principles of the National plan already in partial operation in contemporary industry, politics, and society. There is, indeed, nothing in the National plan which does not already exist as a germ or vigorous shoot in the present order, and this is so simply because Nationalism is evolution.

But perhaps it may be objected that the present government employee may resign when he pleases, that his work is voluntary. The reply in the first place is that his work must, in fact, be regarded as compulsory, inasmuch as he, like all of us, must work or starve. He cannot leave his place unless he can find other work to do, and he would have this liberty under the National plan, with the additional advantage that a national labor exchange would provide all possible facilities for men who desired to change work or location. The National plan is even so elastic that it will permit a man to loaf the rest of his life, after a very brief service, if he shall consent to accept a quarter or half the rate of support of other citizens.

In view of the misapprehensions into which General Walker has fallen, it may be well to state explicitly that the most important analogy between the military system and Nationalism is the fact that the latter places the industrial duty of citizens on the ground on which their military duty already rests. All able-bodied citizens are held bound to fight for the nation, and, on the other hand, the nation is bound to protect all citizens, whether able to fight or not. Nationalism extends this accepted principle to industry, and holds every able-bodied citizen bound to work for the nation, whether with mind or muscle; and, on the other hand, holds the nation bound to guarantee livelihood to every citizen, whether able to work or not. As in military matters the duty to fight is conditioned upon the physical ability, while the right to protection is conditioned only upon citizenship, so we would condition the obligation to work upon the strength to work, but the right to support upon citizenship only.

It would, indeed, appear that in using the military analogy I had unwittingly set a snare in divers ways for General Walker, for he says in another place:

"In Mr. Bellamy's army all are to be paid alike, and are to enjoy equivalent physical conditions. The officers and privates are to fare in all respects the same, the highest having no preference whatever over the meanest, absolutely no material consideration being awarded to the greatest powers in production or in administration. Now, the rule is very different from this in the real armies of the civilized world, and Mr. Bellamy would do well to be careful, lest, in leaving out the principle of graded rewards corresponding to gradations of rank, he should omit a feature which may cause his industrial army to fall to pieces."

A considerable experience of criticisms of "Looking Backward" by gentlemen who had been prevented by press of more important business from reading the book had prepared me for some curious statements of what I had put in and what I had left out; but I was distinctly startled to learn that the principle of graded rewards corresponding to ranks had been left out of the constitution of what General Walker calls "Mr. Bellamy's army." Upon consulting the book again, I was pleased to find that my recollection of it was correct, and that, in fact, a special and characteristic feature of the industrial army is such a system of "rewards corresponding to gradations of rank" as makes diligence and achievement in the public service the sole and sure avenue to all social distinction, posts of authority, and honors of office.

It is quite true that the provision for the physical needs of all is the same, because those needs are the same, and because it is a vital principle of Nationalism that all forms of necessary work, from the scavenger's to the statesman's, are equally worthy. The question which arises on this misunderstanding as to the use of terms is whether General Walker fairly represents public sentiment in ruling out any kind of reward or incentive, except money, as effectual. I submit that he is not a fair representative in this respect of the sentiment of men in general, nor even probably of his own serious second thought. Does he think that it is the difference between the salary of the lieutenant and the captain, or the honor and authority of the superior rank, which constitute the chief element in the ambitious dreams of the subaltern? Will he assert, that if the difference in the pay of different ranks from lieutenant to major-general were greatly reduced, there would be a corresponding diminution in the military spirit of the army? Does he argue that the Prussian soldier would prize his iron cross the more if it were made of gold? or can he imagine that the Englishman would be stimulated by offering a lump sum for valor, instead of the Victoria cross?

So long as the nations of which armies are parts are made up of ranks divided by the money line, the pay of officers naturally increases with rank, but the principle, so far from being essential to the spirit of the military career, is, so far as it is influential, injurious to it.

Evidently bred of the same spirit that moves General Walker to suggest that the motive of the soldier is, after all, at bottom a sordid one, is the following:

"Mr. Bellamy's assumption that, were selfish pecuniary interests altogether removed as a motive to action, the sense of duty and the desire of applause would inspire all the members of the community to the due exertion of all their powers and faculties for the general good, is purely gratuitous."

In the first place, this is a misstatement of the case. I nowhere say or imply that the sense of duty and the desire of applause alone will influence all men sufficiently. As has just been explained, the rewards of authority, of social rank and public prominence, are held out to workers as the prizes of diligence, in a manner in which they never have been brought to bear upon human nature under any industrial or social system before, since the world began. The only incentives which are eliminated under the National plan are the desire of inordinate wealth and the fear of poverty.

But it is in vain that we pile up other motives in place of the lust of gold and the fear of want. General Walker refuses to allow that any other motives than these are capable of moving men to any adequate degree. "From the origin of mankind, to the present time," he says, "the main spur to exertion has been want."

Did General Walker ever employ a tramp who was working on an empty stomach for something to fill it? Did he find that such work, where the spur was purely and solely want, was a profitable sort of labor? Has he not found, on the contrary, that the work of a man who has a home, money in the bank, and an insurance on his life, a man with whom want is out of any immediate consideration, is worth five times as much per hour as that of the tramp whom he would apparently have us accept as the ideal laborer? Want, indeed, so far from being the main spur to work, is the motive of only the worst work, while good work is done in the proportion in which fear of want is absent, and the instinct of self-development, of ambition and honor, reputation and power, takes its place. In no way is the impotence of want as a spur to exertion more strikingly illustrated than in its failure to stimulate precisely those classes of society which feel it most.

There are thousands of wretched beings in this and every other country, life-long idlers, paupers, vagabonds, who will starve, freeze, and endure every pang sooner than accept work, even when it is offered to them. Is it asked what Nationalism will do with this class? The answer is straight and swift. It will do with them what the present order cannot do; it will make them work. Equality of rights means equality of duty, and in undertaking to guarantee the one the nation will undertake to enforce the other.

General Walker accuses me of militarism. I confess an admiration of the soldier's business as the only one in which, from the start, men throw away the purse and reject every sordid standard of merit and achievement. The very conditions which Nationalism promises—that is to say, security as to livelihood, with duty and the love of honor as motives—are the actual conditions of military life. Is it a wonder that war has a glamour? That glamour we would give to the peaceful pursuits of industry by making them, like the duty of the soldier, public service. Some have said that Nationalism requires a change in human nature; but men on turning soldiers do not become better men, do not experience a change of heart. They are merely placed under the influence of different incentives. Make industry a public service, as war now is, and you will win for work the inspiration of war.

For the portion of General Walker's argument next to be taken up, I bespeak particular attention. He observes:

"Were the phantasy of a state in which every one should have enough and to spare, in which the conditions of life should cease to be arduous and stern, from which care and solicitude for the future should be banished, and the necessaries, comforts, and wholesome luxuries of life should come easily to all—were this wild, weak dream shown to be capable of realization, well may philanthropists exclaim: 'Alas, for humankind!' There have been races that have lived without care, without struggle, without pains, but that have not become noble races. Except for care and struggle and pains, men would never have risen above the intellectual and physical stature of Polynesians."

I would ask General Walker whether this "wild, weak dream" of a state in which we should have enough and to spare of necessaries and reasonable luxuries, with agreeable conditions of labor and no anxiety about the future, is not precisely the ideal which all of us spend our days and nights in trying to realize for the benefit of ourselves, our families, our children, and our relatives. Would General Walker teach us that in seeking this ideal for ourselves and those dear to us we run the risk of becoming Polynesians? Probably not. Well, now, the whole Nationalist proposition is merely that, instead of seeking this ideal every man for himself and the devil for us all, and thereby for the most part missing it quite, we unite our efforts, and by combined and concerted action command success for all. General Walker's point, then, appears to be that while the effort to better our condition is commendable, and even a matter of duty, so long as it is pursued individually, by the method of mutual hindrance, it becomes Polynesian the moment the method of mutual assistance and cooperation is adopted. I think the reader will admit that I do not exaggerate in claiming this passage of General Walker's argument as the most extraordinary and purely original contribution to social science which has recently been made.

"There are cares that cark and kill," pursues General Walker, with a feeling that makes me suspect he is, after all, a Nationalist at heart; "there are struggles that are unavailing; there are pains that depress and blight and dwarf. Well may we look forward"—(surely the man is a Nationalist)—"to a better state, in which much of the harshness of the human condition shall, by man's own efforts, have been removed. But it was no Bellamy who said that in the sweat of their brows should men eat bread." Quite right, General. All Bellamy said was that they should not eat their bread in the sweat of other people's brows.

In discussing the feasibility of a central national con-

trol of the entire working force of the country, General
Walker says: "The greatest practical difficulty in the
application of this principle would be in equalizing the
advantages of country and city life." His fear is that
under Nationalism nobody would be willing to live in
the country, and consequently there would be a general
rush to the cities. It seems very evident to me that
General Walker would never have raised this point had
he not become temporarily mixed up as to which side he
held a brief for. Surely no one can know better than
General Walker that it is precisely in this matter of equalizing the advantages of country with city life that the
present industrial system has scored one of its most complete and signal failures. The abandonment of the farm
for the town is conceded to be one of the most alarming
features of the present social situation. What on earth
was General Walker thinking of to call attention to the
fact that, at the present rate of the rush cityward, the
abandonment of the country bids fair to be completed
long before the Nationalists have a chance to try their
hands? Could there be a more striking illustration, if for
the purpose of the figure we may identify General Walker with the system he defends, of a man with an actual
and colossal beam in his own eye animadverting upon a
theoretical mote in somebody's else?

Meanwhile it serves our purpose that General Walker
should have raised this point, for it gives me an opportunity to remark that a direct tendency of Nationalism
will be to check the excessive growth of the cities at the
expense of the country. A central control of production
and distribution will, to a great degree, destroy the ad-

vantages which, under the competitive system, great cities have over villages as localities for manufacturing, and the result will be industrial, and as a consequence social, decentralization. The cooperative features of the National plan will, indeed, greatly increase the pleasures and conveniences of city life, but not relatively more than they will enhance the attractions of life in the village.

I shall now take up the severest charge which General Walker makes against Nationalism. He says that what he justly calls "the fundamental proposition of Nationalism," namely, that all workers shall share alike in the national product, is "dishonest." That there may be no doubt as to his position, he adds that "to say that one who produces twice as much as another shall yet have no more is palpable robbery. It is to make that man for half his time a slave working for others without reward."

Here we have a very explicit statement that the producer should have what he produces, and, as a necessary consequence, that the non-producer should have nothing, for evidently, if the producer has all he produces, there will be nothing left for the non-producer. Moreover, if it be "dishonest" for the weak worker to share equally with the strong, it would obviously be still more so for the idler to get anything at all. Now, under the present industrial system it is tolerably notorious that the hardest workers and chiefest producers are the poorest paid and worst treated, while not only do idlers share their product with them, but get the lion's share of it. Is General Walker willing that the present industrial system shall be remodeled on the plan he lays down as the only honest one—of giving the whole product to the producer? If so, the Anarchists are to be congratulated upon the ardor of their new disciple. If not, he certainly owes an explanation to the friends of the present industrial system for giving away their case so completely.

Let me suggest that his explanation may be very simple. Instead of the word "produces," he should have used the phrase "can get hold of." This simple change makes all the difference in the world. To say a man is entitled to what he "produces" is to invite instant revolution; but to say that a man is entitled to what he "can get hold of" is to state the fundamental principle of the present order.

Meanwhile I will briefly mention the grounds on which Nationalism insists that the weak worker shall share equally with the stronger, or, to put it more broadly, that all men and women, while required to render such service as they may be capable of, shall share alike this total product. This law results from the fact that Nationalism contemplates society, both economically and morally, not as an accidental conglomeration of mutually independent and unconnected molecules, but as an organism, not complete in its molecules, but in its totality only. It refuses to recognize the individual as standing alone, or as living or working to or for himself alone, but insists upon regarding him as an inseparable member of humanity, with an allegiance and a duty to his fellows which he could not, if he would, cast off, and with claims upon his fellows which are equally obligatory upon them. In a word, Nationalism holds that every one is born into the world a debtor to society for all he can do, a creditor to society for all he needs. It proposes a plan by which this great exchange of duties, this discharge of reciprocal responsibilities, may be effected.

Perhaps General Walker will be able to see that with this plan, which counts all human beings equal partners in a business carried on from generation to generation, from the beginning of humanity to the end of the world, and indefinitely further, the practice of Saturday-night settlements between the members of the firm, with mutual handwashings as to further responsibilities for one another, would scarcely be consistent.

A defect of General Walker's method as a social philosopher is that he overworks his savages and Polynesians as illustrations, when he could easily find much more pertinent analogies in the community about him, if he would only look around a little. For example, in going on to argue that a uniform rate of compensation is ruinous, he says, "Such a levelling downwards would end all progress," and adds that there are plenty of tribes and races in which it is in full operation. Unfortunately for Nationalism, he remarks, "They are all miserable embruted savages." Now, the trade-unions of America and England are, to a very large extent, based upon the principle of a uniform scale of wages, and on this basis have been doing the world's work for a long time. It will, doubtless, be a painful surprise to them, and, indeed, to the communities whose work they do, to learn that they are "all miserable embruted savages." Is not General Walker a trifle harsh?

The limits of this article compel me to pass on to that portion of General Walker's paper in which he discusses

the aims and ends of the Nationalist party. He com-
plains that he finds no statement of the means by which
Nationalists propose to accomplish their end of having
all industries operated in the interest of and by the nation. Now, I may be permitted to say that it is entirely General Walker's own fault if he does not know just
the steps by which Nationalists propose to make a beginning in carrying out their programme. In public addresses, in articles published in recognized organs of the
movement, and in hearings before legislative committees,
there has been no lack of explicit statements on this subject from the beginning of the movement. In this respect,
indeed, its history from the start has been a practical
refutation of the charge of being impractical, brought
against it by sundry critics who have not cared to know
the truth.

In the next place, I must correct a serious misstatement made by General Walker. He says in a footnote
to his article:

"While the hero of the book goes to sleep in 1887
and wakes in 2,000 the new state has been in perfect
operation for a long time. The great change is spoken
of as having taken place instantaneously, through the
simple formation of the industrial army."

This statement is wholly without foundation. In the sermon of Dr. Barton the change is described as having
been effected "in the time of one generation," and else-
where is spoken of as having been completed "early in
the twentieth century." There is nowhere in the book the
slightest foundation for General Walker's declaration that
"the great change is spoken of as having taken place in-

stantaneously through the simple formation of the industrial army." It has always been my own belief, and I think that of Nationalists in general, that, always subject to the leading of events, the process of the nationalization of industry will be gradual, first embracing certain semipublic businesses and extending to others as indicated by their special conditions; the controlling idea being always to avoid derangement of business and undue hardship to individuals. Confiscation is not a method of Nationalism.

For the benefit of those who may share the self-inflicted ignorance of General Walker, I will briefly state what, to begin with, Nationalists propose. First and foremost, they favor an immediate and radical improvement in the school system of the country, which shall give the children of the poor equal advantages with those of the rich, so far as regards the public school system. In the schoolroom they would begin to build the new nation. To this end they propose raising the limit of compulsory education year by year, as rapidly as public sentiment will permit. They propose making the compulsory period for all children cover the entire period during which the schools are open, instead of a part of it, as, for example, in Massachusetts a beggarly twenty weeks in the year, the schools being open nearly twice that time. They propose to make the employment of children during term time or school hours a misdemeanor. In cases of great poverty they propose such provision for the partial support of children as may be necessary to enable them to attend school.

The Nationalists propose the immediate assumption by

the municipalities of the heating, lighting, and surface and elevated car lines of towns, with all other services now performed by corporations. They oppose and protest against the granting of any more public franchises to individuals or corporations under any circumstances. Let the people attend to their own business. They propose the nationalization of telephones and telegraphs, and the assumption of the express business by the post-office. They propose national control of the railroads of the country. They propose that all mineral deposits hereafter discovered or opened shall belong to the nation. They propose national control of all coal mines now in operation.

A body of 1,500,000 workingmen would by these measures be taken into the public service. It is proposed that this force should be organized on a thoroughly humane basis of steady employment, reasonable hours, pensions for sickness, accident, and age, with liability to discharge only for fault or incompetence after a fair hearing.

A specific plan is proposed by which political executives would be deprived of influence through patronage over the industrial service, and its abuse for partisan ends rendered impossible.

It is claimed that the public control of these branches of business would result not only in the great betterment of the condition of the employees, but also in far greater cheapness and efficiency of service. Take the single instance of the coal business. Instead of shutting down the mines whenever the demand temporarily slackens, and putting up prices as soon as it starts up again, the government would work the mines continuously to their

# EDWARD BELLAMY SPEAKS AGAIN!

full capacity. Instead of piling up the product at tide-water to clog transportation at any increase of demand, and thus excuse extortionate prices, the coal would be forwarded as fast as mined to distributing centers all over the country, from which consumer could be promptly and conveniently served. The price of coal under these conditions would never exceed the figures represented by the cost of mining and the actual freight under favorable transportation conditions, nor, with suitable accumulations at the distributing points, need it vary between winter and summer, or between mild and severe seasons.

Lack of space forbids me to dwell upon the effect to purge our legislative and congressional lobbies, to put an end to stock-gambling in its chief form, and to terminate the wholesale swindling of the investing public by railroad promoters, speculators, grabbers, and wreckers, which would result from nationalizing the railroads.

# Why I Wrote "Looking Backward"

## By Edward Bellamy

*(From The Nationalist, May, 1890)*

I ACCEPT more readily the invitation to tell in The Nationalist how I came to write "Looking Backward" for the reason that it will afford an opportunity to clear up certain points on which inquiries have been frequently addressed to me. I never had, previous to the publication of the work, any affiliations with any class or sect of industrial or social reformers nor, to make my confession complete, any particular sympathy with undertakings of the sort. It is only just to myself to say, however, that this should not be taken to indicate any indifference to the miserable condition of the mass of humanity, seeing that it resulted rather from a perception all too clear of the depth and breadth of the social problem and a consequent skepticism as to the effectiveness of the proposed solutions which had come to my notice.

In undertaking to write "Looking Backward" I had, at the outset, no idea of attempting a serious contribution to the movement of social reform. The idea was of a mere literary fantasy, a fairy tale of social felicity. There was no thought of contriving a house which practical men might live in, but merely of hanging in mid-air, far out of reach of the sordid and material world of the present, a cloud-palace for an ideal humanity.

199

# EDWARD BELLAMY SPEAKS AGAIN!

In order to secure plenty of elbow room for the fancy and prevent awkward collisions between the ideal structure and the hard facts of the real world, I fixed the date of the story in the year A. D. 3000. As to what might be in A. D. 3000 one man's opinion was as good as another's, and my fantasy of the social system of that day only required to be consistent with itself to defy criticism. Emboldened by the impunity my isolated position secured me, I was satisfied with nothing less than the whole earth for my social palace. In its present form the story is a romance of the ideal nation, but in its first form it was a romance of an ideal world. In the first draft of "Looking Backward," though the immediate scene was laid in America (in Asheville, North Carolina, instead of Boston, by the way,) the United States was supposed to be merely an administrative province of the great World Nation, whose affairs were directed from the World Capital which was declared to be the city of Berne, in Switzerland. The action of the story was made to begin in the thirtieth century.

The opening scene was a grand parade of a departmental division of the industrial army on the occasion of the annual muster day when the young men coming of age that year were mustered into the national service and those who that year had reached the age of exemption were mustered out. That chapter always pleased me and it was with some regrets that I left it out of the final draft. The solemn pageantry of the great festival of the year, the impressive ceremonial of the oath of duty taken by the new recruits in presence of the world-standard, the formal return of the thanks of humanity to the veterans who received their honorable dismissal from service, the review and march past of the entire body of the local industrial forces, each battalion with its appropriate insignia, the triumphal arches, the garlanded streets, the banquets, the music, the open theatres and pleasure gardens, with all the features of a gala day sacred to the civic virtues and the enthusiasm of humanity, furnished materials for a picture exhilarating at least to the painter.

The idea of committing the duty of maintaining the community to an industrial army, precisely as the duty of protecting it is entrusted to a military army, was directly suggested to me by the grand object lesson of the organization of an entire people for national purposes presented by the military system of universal service for fixed and equal terms, which has been practically adopted by the nations of Europe and theoretically adopted everywhere else as the only just and only effectual plan of public defense on a great scale. What inference could possibly be more obvious and more unquestionable than the advisability of trying to see if a plan which was found to work so well for purposes of destruction might not be profitably applied to the business of production now in such shocking confusion. But while this idea had for some time been vaguely floating in my mind, for a year or two I think at least, I had been far from realizing all that was in it, and only thought then of utilizing it as an analogy to lend an effect of feasibility to the fancy sketch I had in hand. It was not till I began to work out the details of the scheme by way of explaining how the people of the thirtieth century disposed of the awkward problems of labor and avoided the evils of a classified society that I perceived the full potency of the instrument I was using and recognized in the modern military system not merely a rhetorical analogy for a national industrial service, but its prototype, furnishing at once a complete working model for its organization, an arsenal of patriotic and national motives and arguments for its animation, and the unanswerable demonstration of its feasibility drawn from the actual experience of whole nations organized and manoeuvred as armies.

Something in this way it was that, no thanks to myself, I stumbled over the destined corner-stone of the new social order. It scarcely needs to be said that having once apprehended it for what it was, it became a matter of pressing importance to me to show it in the same light to other people. This led to a complete recasting, both in form and purpose, of the book I was engaged upon. Instead of a mere fairy tale of social perfection, it became the vehicle of a definite scheme of industrial reorganization. The form of a romance was retained, although with some impatience, in the hope of inducing the more to give it at least a reading. Barely enough story was left to decently drape the skeleton of the argument and not enough, I fear, in spots, for even that purpose. A great deal of merely fanciful matter concerning the manners, customs, social and political institutions, mechanical contrivances, and so forth of the people of the thirtieth century, which had been intended for the book, was cut out for fear of diverting the attention of readers from the main theme. Instead of the year A. D. 3000, that of A. D. 2000 was fixed upon as the date of the story. Ten centuries had at first seemed to me none too much to allow for the evolution of anything like an ideal society, but with my new belief as to the part which the National organization of industry is to play in bringing in the good time coming, it appeared to me reasonable to suppose that by the year 2000 the order of things which we look forward to will already have become an exceedingly old story. This conviction as to the shortness of the time in which the hope of Nationalization is to be realized by the birth of the new, and the first true, nation, I wish to say, is one which every day's reflection and observation, since the publication of "Looking Backward," has tended to confirm.

The same clearer conviction as to the method by which this great change is to come about, which caused me to shorten so greatly my estimate of the time in which it was to be accomplished, necessitated the substitution of the conception of a separate national evolution for the original idea of a homogeneous world-wide social system. The year 3000 may, indeed, see something of that sort, but not the year 2000. It would be preposterous to assume parity of progress between America and Turkey. The more advanced nations, ours surely first of all, will reach the summit earliest and, reaching strong brotherly hands downward, help up the laggards.

# Fourth of July, 1992

*(By Edward Bellamy in Boston Globe, July 4, 1892\*)*

IN THE year 1992, it is safe to say, the Fourth of July will have ceased to be a popular holiday of much note.

Somewhere between today and the Fourth of July, 1992, there will be another Declaration of Independence in America, which, in importance, will quite eclipse the document (great in its way as that was), which was promulgated at Philadelphia 116 years ago.

Our descendants, as intelligent students of history, will no doubt give due recognition to the work done that day, as a necessary step in the national evolution, but they will not the less marvel in their hearts at the exceeding simplicity of a people who could consider themselves free and independent, merely because as states they had sundered certain political ties with a foreign state, while retaining for the regulation of their mutual relations as individuals an economic system based on inequalities of wealth which made the many dependents and suppliants of the few for all the means of life and happiness, and even for the opportunity to stand upon the earth and toil.

The new declaration of independence which I predict, will not deal with the relations of this country with other

---

*Reprinted by special permission from The Boston Globe.

countries, but with the relations of the people of this country with one another.

It will abolish for all time the distinctions of master-ship and servitude, employer and employed, capitalist and proletarian, and declare every man forevermore inde-pendent of every other man and every woman of every man.

It will put an end to economic inequality as the root of all injustice and proclaim the industrial republic wherein all the citizens shall be equal co-operators in producing the means of life and enjoyment and equal sharers in the results.

On what day of what month of what year this new and greater declaration of independence will come I am not so presumptuous as to predict, but I believe it will come and that society will be, peaceably or forcibly, con-formed to its terms within the expectation of life of men now middle-aged.

Seeing then that our present little Fourth of July is so soon to pass into comparative obscuration, let us make the most of it while we have it, piously remembering that had not our fathers worked the deliverance they did in their day, their posterity would not be able to work the greater deliverance that is now at hand.

# Should Every Boy Learn a Trade?
## And How Shall He Find Out What He Is Best Fitted For?

*(Contributed by Edward Bellamy to symposium in Boston Herald, August 9, 1892\*)*

I F EVERY boy learned a trade, none of them would be better off, because under the present industrial system there is always and necessarily a large margin of unemployed. It would make no difference as to this margin of unemployed whether all workmen were skilled in trades or all unskilled. The proportion of unemployed would, on the whole, be larger if all workmen were skilled, because in that case it might be presumed that the total product would be greater, and it is the difficulty of getting rid of the product which under the present industrial system limits employment.

As a general proposition, it would, therefore, in no way help the situation if every boy were to learn a trade, for the total number of the unemployed would be more rather than less. As a personal and particular proposition, it may help some boys to learn trades, so long as other boys do not, for it might give them a little better chance as against the others, in the competition for work. The question is, therefore, one of interest only as an element in a personal and selfish calculation.

*Reprinted by special permission from The Boston Herald.

# EDWARD BELLAMY SPEAKS AGAIN!

If every American boy were graduated from school with a trade perfectly acquired, it would not lessen the number of unemployed or the misery of their condition, except as it might give this country an advantage over foreign countries in the cheapness of skilled labor, and, therefore, increase the misery of the workers in such countries, to the advantage chiefly, and at last wholly, of the capitalists in this country.

Under the national co-operative system of industry advocated by nationalists, the situation would be entirely different. That system would give to every citizen a right to consume an equal share of the total national product, and the only limit to the consumption of products would therefore be the satisfaction of all wants.

As to the second question, the only possible reply is that under the present social and industrial system it is out of the question for a young man to determine in any way, except by natural intuition or by hard knocks, what pursuit he is adapted for. No trade or profession welcomes him, for under the competitive system it is the interest of workers in every occupation to have as few competitors for employment or patronage as possible. The young man coming into active life, and seeking something to do, finds every line of business closed against him as tight as a clam, and he can only hope to get into any by breaking in.

So it always has been and always will be until nationalism comes. Then every fresh brain and every new pair of hands will be welcomed to the army of industry, for then none will fight for himself any more than the individual soldier fights for himself, but each for all and all for each.

Then all will share equally in the total product of all trades, and the only motive for seeking one trade rather than another will be one's liking and aptitude for it; and because each will be most efficient in the work he likes best it will be the policy of the nation to provide every possible means for testing any special faculties anyone may think he possesses, in order that he may find the place in which he can, while best contenting himself, be most useful to the joint concern.

The one trade every boy and girl should learn today is the trade of a nationalist preacher, in order that a state of things may be brought about which shall secure work and comfort to all.

# The Outcome of the Battle of Standards

(*Edward Bellamy in the Boston Globe, Sunday, July 16, 1893, on the question: "Will gold become the sole unit of value, and will silver cease to be used as money?"**)

T HIS question is merely an aspect of a larger one, namely, whether the money power is to grow to complete mastery or not. The interest of the monopolizers of money is in having its value as high as possible and its supply as small as possible, since thereby their control of the world by its means is made more complete, inevitable and easy of exercise. The movement toward the gold standard is a part of the great modern tendency to the centralization of the economic government of the world in the hands of a few.

The resistance to the gold unit in the interest of a bimetallic or broader basis and larger money supply represents an effort of the people to repel this tendency and resist this domination. It is democratic and popular in sentiment and breathes the spirit of resistance to tyranny. Is it, then, to be a successful resistance? I must say that, while I heartily sympathize with it and will do all I can to further it, I doubt if it will be in the end successful, and this not at all for moral but entirely for what may be called strategic reasons.

As I said, the gold unit movement is a part of the great modern tendency to suppress the free competitive system in the interest of centralized and combined economic ad-

---

*Reprinted by special permission from The Boston Globe.

211

ministration. In resisting it the bi-metallic or broader money basis party is, in strict economic terms, necessarily arrayed in defense of the old-fashioned free competitive system.

Now, while the free competitive system would be vastly better than the centralized despotism of capital which the bi-metallic party is resisting, it is a doomed and dying system to which the world will never return. Capitalistic oppression, using the new and all-conquering method of concentration, cannot therefore be successfully resisted from behind the decayed and dilapidated breastworks of free competition.

The forces arrayed on the popular side of this money standard struggle may make a more or less stubborn battle, but they will eventually be forced to surrender unless they take the higher ground of nationalism. The only way to meet the method of concentration applied in the interest of the few is by applying the same method in the interest of the people. Modern artillery cannot be met by ancient ordnance.

So we may be sure in the end the battle between the money standards will become a battle between the present social system and a system that will need no money standard, because it will not measure men's rights that way. The money problem will never be solved; it will be abolished. Money is the root of all evil, and can never be made to grow straight or bear anything but apples of Sodom. It will never be effectually treated save by extirpation. Gold will not conquer silver, nor silver gold but men will conquer both and put them under their feet.

# How to Employ the Unemployed!

## Should the State or Municipality Provide Work for Its Unemployed?

### By Edward Bellamy

*(From Boston Traveler, Nov. 4, 1893\*)*

THE operation of the plan would be something as follows: Let us say there are 1000 or 10,000 unemployed able-bodied persons having a legal settlement in this state, who desire work. Out of this number a certain proportion can make shoes, others can spin or weave, others can make garments, others can build houses and do blacksmithing and others can farm and take care of live-stock, while many more without trades are capable of common labor of any sort. Now, these men and women do not need any one to provide for them; they do not need charity from the state or anybody else. All they need, in order to be fed, clothed and sheltered is to be set to work to support one another. Stick a pin here. The idea is that they are to support one another. They are to consume one another's products. State product is not to be sold or to go into the general market at all to compete with wage-produced goods or with private employers, but to be consumed wholly within the group of previously unemployed workers. Now, here is where the function of the state comes in.

---

\*Reprinted by special permission from the Boston Traveler.

# EDWARD BELLAMY SPEAKS AGAIN!

State workers need to be organized and provided with tools, in order to support one another, and they cannot organize themselves. This it is proper to expect the state to do, both for the welfare of an unfortunate class of citizens, and also for the protection of the public treasury from the burden of supporting them by alms, which must otherwise fall on it. It will be observed that this is not a question of charity; for the incapable, the almshouses would remain. It is merely the question of putting the able-bodied persons in a position to support themselves. The idea is to furnish the necessary machinery to utilize an existing power which otherwise will run to waste. The state would be at expense to provide the necessary farms, manufacturing plants and buildings, and, for a time, until the products began to come in, it would have to keep the workers; but, after that, the system would be self-sustaining.

In this brief space I can but mention a few points of the plan, viz: In the first place, it contemplates a permanent establishment, for it is nonsense to regard the problem of the unemployed as anything but a permanent problem. This establishment would undoubtedly always be in operation, although the number dependent on it would increase and decrease according to the times. It would be an elastic system, and after it was in full adjustment a man or woman out of work could get work for a week, a month or a year, as they chose. The establishment would not need to be concentrated, but its different branches might be scattered. In each settlement there would be the farm or factory, the dwellings and the store. This store would be wholly stocked with products of the workers, although at first the state would have to furnish many deficiencies. The workers would from the first be guaranteed a decent and sufficient maintenance, nothing more. For this purpose they would be supplied with a sort of scrip, good only at the public store and for lodging at the public dwellings; the allowance for each worker would invariably be equal and the same.

After the expense of the state superintendence and other outlays was provided for, the total product would be divided in the form of scrip among the workers, so that as the total product increased the rate of maintenance would increase, the system being one of co-operation under state superintendence and guarantee. The workers should be regarded as in no way objects of charity or wards of the state, but, while subject to strict working rules, should in all other respects be as independent as other citizens.

While the state works would be intended, at the outset, to attract only the needy unemployed, it is probable that the advantages resulting from security of employment and the steady rise in rate of maintenance which would follow the increasing efficiency of the system, would suffice not only to retain all who once entered this co-operative service, but to raise the condition of labor generally by compelling private employers to bid against a fair and humane system of employment in order to obtain workers.

# How I Wrote "Looking Backward"

### By Edward Bellamy

### (*From The Ladies Home Journal, April, 1894\**)

U P TO the age of eighteen I had lived almost continually in a thriving village of New England, where
there were no very rich and very few poor, and everybody who was willing to work was sure of a fair living.
At that time I visited Europe and spent a year there in
travel and study. It was in the great cities of England,
Europe, and among the hovels of the peasantry that my
eyes were first fully opened to the extent and consequences of man's inhumanity to man.

I well remember in those days of European travel how
much more deeply that blue background of misery im-
pressed me than the palaces and cathedrals in relief
against it. I distinctly recall the innumerable debates,
suggested by the piteous sights about us, which I had with
a dear companion of my journey, as to the possibility of
finding some great remedy for poverty, some plan for
equalizing human conditions. Our discussions usually
brought up against the same old stump: who would do
the dirty work? We did not realize, as probably few do
who lightly dismiss the subject of social reform with the
same query, that its logic implies the condonation of all

forms of slavery. Not until we all acknowledge the
world's "dirty work" as our common and equal responsibility, shall we be in a position intelligently to consider,
or have the disposition seriously to seek a just and reasonable way of distributing and adjusting the burden.
So it was that I returned home, for the first time aroused
to the existence and urgency of the social problem, but
without as yet seeing any way out. Although it had required the sights of Europe to startle me to a vivid realization of the inferno of poverty beneath our civilization,
my eyes having once been opened I had now no difficulty
in recognizing in America, and even in my own comparatively prosperous village, the same conditions in
course of progressive development.

The other day rummaging among old papers I was
much interested by the discovery of some writings indicative of my state of mind at that period. If the reader will glance over the following extracts from the manu-
script of an address which it appears I delivered before
the Chicopee Falls Village Lyceum along in 1871 or 1872,
he will probably admit that their youthful author was
quite likely to attempt something in the line of "Looking Backward" if he only lived long enough. The subject
of this address was "The Barbarism of Society," the barbarism being held to consist in and result from inequality in the distribution of wealth. From numerous equally
radical expressions I excerpt these paragraphs: "The
great reforms of the world have hitherto been political
rather than social. In their progress classes privileged
by title have been swept away, but classes privileged by
wealth remain. A nominal aristocracy is ceasing to ex-

218

ist, but the actual aristocracy of wealth, the world over, is every day becoming more and more powerful. The idea that men can derive a right from birth or name to dispose of the destinies of their fellows is exploded, but the world thinks not yet of denying that gold confers a power upon its possessors to domineer over their equals and enforce from them a life's painful labors at the price of a bare subsistence. I would not have indignation blind my eyes or confuse my reason in the contemplation of this injustice, but I ask you what is the name of an institution by which men control the labor of other men, and out of the abundance created by that labor having doled out to the laborers such a pittance as may barely support life and sustain strength for added tasks, reserve to themselves the vast surplus for the support of a life of ease and splendor? This, gentlemen, is slavery; a slavery whose prison is the world, whose shackles and fetters are the unyielding frame of society, whose lash is hunger, whose taskmasters are those bodily necessities for whose supply the rich who hold the keys of the world's granaries must be appealed to, and the necks of the needy bowed to their yoke as the price of the boon of life. . . . Consider a moment the condition of that class of society by whose unremitting toil the ascendancy of man over the material universe is maintained and his existence rendered possible on earth, remembering, also, that this class comprises the vast majority of the race. Born of parents whom brute passion impelled to the propagation of their kind; bred in penury and the utter lack of all those luxuries and amenities of life which go so far to make existence tolerable; their intellectual faculties neglected and an unnatural and forced development given to their basest instincts; their childhood, the sweet vacation of life, saddened and deadened by the pinching of poverty, and then, long before the immature frame could support the severity of labor, forced from the playground into the factory or field! Then begins the obscure, uninteresting drama of a laborer's life; an unending procession of toilsome days relieved by brief and rare holidays and harassed by constant anxiety lest he lose all he claims from the world—a place to labor. He feels, in some dumb, unreasoning way, oppressed by the frame of society, but it is too heavy for him to lift. The institutions that crush him down assume to his dulled brain the inevitable and irresistible aspect of natural laws. And so, with only that dim sense of injustice which no subtlety of reasoning, no array of argument can banish from the human soul when it feels itself oppressed, he bows his head to his fate.

"Let not any one falsely reply that I am dreaming of a happiness without toil, of abundance without labor. Labor is the necessary condition, not only of abundance but of existence upon earth. I ask only that none labor beyond measure that others may be idle, that there be no more masters and no more slaves among men. Is this too much? Does any fearful soul exclaim, impossible, that this hope has been the dream of men in all ages, a shadowy and Utopian reverie of a divine fruition which the earth can never bear? That the few must revel and the many toil; the few waste, the many want; the few be masters, the many serve; the toilers of the earth be the poor and the idlers the rich, and that this must go on forever?

# HOW I WROTE "LOOKING BACKWARD"

"Ah, no; has the world then dreamed in vain. Have the ardent longings of the lovers of men been toward an unattainable felicity? Are the aspirations after liberty, equality and happiness implanted in the very core of our hearts for nothing?

"Not so, for nothing that is unjust can be eternal and nothing that is just can be impossible."

Since I came across this echo of my youth and recalled the half-forgotten exercises of mind it testifies to, I have been wondering, not why I wrote "Looking Backward," but why I did not write it, or try to twenty years ago.

Like most men, however, I was under the sordid and selfish necessity of solving the economic problem in its personal bearings before I could give much time to the cure of society in general. I had, like others, to fight my way to a place at the world's work-bench where I could make a living. For a dozen or fifteen years I followed journalism, doing in a desultory way, as opportunity offered, a good deal of magazine and book writing. In none of the writings of this period did I touch on the social question, but not the less all the while it was in mind, as a problem not by any means given up, how poverty might be abolished and the economic equality of all citizens of the republic be made as much a matter of course as their political equality. I had always the purpose, some time when I had sufficient leisure, to give myself earnestly to the examination of this great problem, but meanwhile kept postponing it, giving my time and thoughts to easier tasks.

Possibly I never should have mustered up courage for an undertaking so difficult and indeed so presumptuous, but for events which gave the problem of life a new and more solemn meaning to me. I refer to the birth of my children.

I confess I cannot understand the mental operations of good men or women who from the moment they are parents do not become intensely interested in the social question. That an unmarried man or even a man childless though married should concern himself little about the future of a race in which he may argue that he will have no personal stake, is conceivable, though such indifference is not morally edifying.

From the time their children are born it becomes the great problem with parents how to provide for and safeguard their future when they themselves shall no longer be on earth. To this end they painfully spare and save and plot and plan to secure for their offspring all the advantages that may give them a better chance than other men's children in the struggle for existence.

They do this, knowing sadly well the while, from observation and experience, how vain all such safeguards may prove, how impossible it is for even the wisest and wealthiest of fathers to make sure that the cherished child he leaves behind may not be glad to earn his bread as a servant to the children of his father's servants. Still the parent toils and saves, feeling that this is the best and all he can do for his offspring, little though it be. But is it? Surely a moment's thought will show that this is a wholly unscientific way of going about the work of providing for the future of one's children.

This is the problem of all problems to which the individualistic method is most inapplicable, the problem be-

fore all others of which the only adequate solution must
necessarily be a social solution. Your fear for your child
is that he may fall into the ditch of poverty or be way-
laid by robbers. So you give him a lantern and provide
him with arms. That would be all very well if you could
not do better, but would it not be an infinitely wiser and
more efficient method to join hands with all the other
equally anxious parents, and fill up the ditch and ex-
terminate the robbers, so that safety might be a matter
of course for all? However high, however wise, however
rich you are, the only way you can surely safeguard your
child from hunger, cold and wretchedness and all the
deprivations, degradations and indignities which poverty
implies, is by a plan that will equally safeguard all
men's children. This principle once recognized, the solution of the social problem becomes a simple matter.
Until it is, no solution is possible.

According to my best recollection it was in the fall of
winter of 1886 that I sat down to my desk with the definite purpose of trying to reason out a method of economic
organization by which the republic might guarantee the
livelihood and material welfare of its citizens on a basis
of equality corresponding to and supplementing their political equality. There was no doubt in my mind that
the proposed study should be in the form of a story.
This was not merely because that was a treatment which
would command greater popular attention than others. In
adventuring in any new and difficult field of speculation
I believe that the student often cannot do better than
to use the literary form of fiction. Nothing outside of
the exact sciences has to be so logical as the thread of a

story, if it is to be acceptable. There is no such test of a false and absurd idea as trying to fit it into a story. You may make a sermon or an essay or a philosophical treatise as illogical as you please and no one know the difference, but all the world is a good critic of a story, for it has to conform to the laws of ordinary probability and commonly observed sequence, of which we are all judges.

The stories that I had written before "Looking Backward" were largely of one sort, namely, the working out of problems, that is to say, attempts to trace the logical consequences of certain assumed conditions. It was natural, therefore, that in this form the plan of "Looking Backward" should present itself to my mind. Given the United States, a republic based upon the equality of all men and conducted by their equal voice, what would the natural and logical way be by which to go about the work of guaranteeing an economic equality to its citizens corresponding with their political equality, but without the present unjust discrimination of sex? From the moment the problem first clearly presented itself to my mind in this way, the writing of the book was the simplest thing in the world.

"Looking Backward" has been frequently called a "fanciful" production. Of course, the notion of a man's being resuscitated after a century's sleep is fanciful, and so, of course, are the various other whimsies about life in the year 2000 necessarily inserted to give color to the picture. The argument of the book is, however, about as little fanciful as possible. It is, as I have said, an attempt to work out logically the results of regulating the national system of production and distribution by the democratic principle of the equal rights of all, determined by the equal voice of all.

I defend as material no feature of the plan which cannot be shown to be in accord with that method.

Mány excellent persons, not without sympathy with the idea of a somewhat more equal distribution of this world's wealth, have objected to the principle of absolute and invariable economic equality underlying the plan developed in "Looking Backward." Many have seemed to think that here was an arbitrary detail that might just as well have been modified by admitting economic inequality in proportion to unequal values of industrial service. So it might have been if the plan had been the fanciful theory they supposed it, but regarding it as the result of a rigid application of the democratic idea to the economic system, no feature of the whole plan is more absolutely a matter of course, a more logical necessity than just that. Political equality, which gives all citizens an equal voice in government, without regard to the great differences between men as to intelligence, public service, personal worth and wealth, is the recognition that the essential dignity of human nature is of an importance transcending all personal attributes and accidents and is, therefore, not to be limited by them. In applying the democratic idea to the economic organization, economic equality, without regard to differences of industrial ability, is necessitated by precisely the same logic which justifies political equality. The two ideas are one and stand or fall together.

Nor is economic equality any more an ethical than a necessary physical consequence of democratic rule extended to the productive and distributive system. Political equals will never legislate economic inequality. Nor should they do so. Self preservation forbids it, for economic inequality presently undermines and nullifies political equality and every other form of equality as well.

Moreover, under any system proportioning wealth distribution to industrial performance, how could women be assured an indefeasible equality with men, and their yoke of economic dependence upon the other sex, with all its related and implied subserviences, be finally broken? Surely no social solution not securely guaranteeing that result could claim to be adequate.

I have stopped by the way to say these few words about the plan of "Looking Backward" as the result of the rigid application of the democratic formula to the social problem, and concerning the feature of absolute economic equality as a necessary effect of that method, because it is in these points and their implications that Nationalism, as suggested by "Looking Backward," is, perhaps, most strongly differentiated from other socialistic solutions.

As to the form of the story, my first notion was, while keeping the resuscitated man as a link between the two centuries, not to make him the narrator, or to write chiefly from his point of view, but rather from that of the twentieth century. This would have admitted of some very interesting effects and about half the story was at first written on that line, but as I became convinced of the practical availability of the social solution I was studying, it became my aim to sacrifice all other effects to the method which would enable me to explain its features most fully, which was manifestly that of presenting everything from the point of view of the representative of the nineteenth century.

I have been very frequently asked if I anticipated any considerable effect from the publication of "Looking Backward," and whether I was not very much surprised at the sensation it produced. I cannot say that I was surprised. If it be asked what was the basis of my expectations, I answer the effect of the writing of the book upon myself. When I first undertook to work out the results of a democratic organization of production and distribution based on the recognition of an equal duty of individual service by all citizens and an equal share by all in the result, according to the analogies of military service and taxation and all other relations between the State and the citizen, I believed indeed, it might be possible on this line to make some valuable suggestions upon the social problem, but it was only as I proceeded with the inquiry that I became fully convinced of the entire adequacy of the principle as a social solution, and, moreover, that the achievement of this solution was to be the next great step in human evolution. It would, indeed, be a most impassive person in whose mind so mighty a hope could grow without producing strong emotions.

Knowing that "as face answereth to face in water, so the heart of man to man," I could not doubt that the hope that moved me must needs, in like manner, move all who should come even in part to share it.

As well as I can remember "Looking Backward" began in earnest to be written in the fall or winter of 1886, and was substantially finished in the following six or eight months, although rewriting and revising took up the following spring and summer. It went to the publishers in August or September, 1887, and although promptly accepted did not appear till January, 1888. Although it made a stir among the critics up to the close of 1888 the sales had not exceeded ten thousand, after which they leaped into the hundred thousands.

# Introduction to "The Fabian Essays"

### By Edward Bellamy

### (*American Edition 1894*)

THE introduction to the American public of the present edition of the deservedly famous English work known as "The Fabian Essays," is an occasion that suggests some general observations upon the subject of socialism, considered especially from the American point of view.

Until very recently socialism has been a word rarely heard in the United States, and still more rarely understood, even among intelligent persons. Till quite lately the average American has conceived of a socialist, when he has considered him at all, as a mysterious type of desperado, reputed to infest the dark places of continental Europe and engaged with his fellows in a conspiracy as monstrous as it was futile, against civilization and all that it implied. That such an atrocious and hopeless undertaking should find any following of sane men, has seemed accountable only by the oppressions of European despots and their maddening effect on the popular mind. That socialism could never take root in a republic like ours was assumed as an axiom. Though it might be well enough for Americans to study the phenomena of socialism, in a philosophic and purely speculative way, as a disease of monarchical systems, any one would have been laughed at who should have suggested ten years ago that the subject would ever have a practical interest to our people.

# EDWARD BELLAMY SPEAKS AGAIN!

That was but yesterday, and today the most significant and important movement of thought among the American people, is agreed by all observers to be the growth of the socialistic sentiment. Today, in this country, the various aspects of radical social and economic reform on socialistic lines are the most prominent themes of literary treatment, of public discussion, and of private debate whenever two or three serious-minded persons take counsel together as to the state of the nation.

At first, when the social question so suddenly seized upon the attention of the American people, there were those who reasoned that the interest in the subject would prove transient; that it was, in fact, but a "fad." There are few, if any, who so delude themselves at this writing. So rapidly has the popular interest in socialistic ideas broadened and deepened, and shown its working in the fields of literature, of legislation, of political organization, that there are today few so purblind as not to see and admit that the social problem, the great problem of social justice here, as in Europe, can be got rid of only by being solved, and, until then, will have no mercy on our peace. Already it is apparent from the shaping of events that the public questions of the coming time are to be social, industrial, humane, and not political and partisan. They are to be concerned, not with the external relations of the nation with other nations, but with the radical analysis and reconstruction of the relations in which classes and individuals within the nation stand toward one another and the whole. More and more all other issues are to be subordinated to and absorbed in the one great issue between the present economic system

230

on the one hand, and a radically new and nobler system on the other. In this great controversy we all who yet have any considerable stretch of life before us must take one side or the other, and the air already is electric with the tension of decision. The elderly men who are about retiring from the stage of public affairs, may be able without too much discredit, provided they are not dilatory, to carry to the grave intact the ignorance of their generation as to socialism, but no branch of education is going to be more essential to the outfit of the rising generation, than a full and discriminating acquaintance with the subject. These are conditions surely which leave no argument necessary as to the public utility of all efforts at the present time to promote the study, by Americans especially, of socialism, or, if we may so translate the term, of humane economics, as contrasted with the political economy of the schools.

At the outset of any such study several general questions are suggested. What is socialism? Why is it so late a comer among the forces of civilization? For while so very newly arisen in America, it has really not been known very much longer (only some fifty years or so) in Europe. Why again, has it come to the front at this particular time in America, and why did it raise its head earlier in Europe? And why have its ideas never in previous ages produced any deep or extended movement among the nations of the world?

For the purpose of these questions socialism may be said to be the application of the democratic method to the economic administration of a people. It aims by substituting public management of industry and commerce in the common interest, for private management in diverse personal interests, to more nearly equalize the distribution of wealth, while at the same time increasing the volume of wealth produced for distribution. This definition while, of course, not going at all into details, will suffice to suggest the answer to the second question raised, namely, Why has socialism been so late a comer among the forces of civilization? It is simply because the democratic idea—the idea of self-government by the people for their own benefit—has only within a very recent period achieved a firm establishment in men's minds. The democratic idea must first be established as a general theory of government, that is, in the political field, before the idea can occur of applying it to the economic field. The democratic movement in Europe, although the French Revolution broke the ground for it, did not effectively begin till the first third and middle of the present century, after the reaction against the Revolution had lost its force. Consequently, we find, as might be expected, the rise of socialism dating from that period. European democracy, almost from the first, took on a socialistic quality for the reason that the pressing economic misery of the people suggested as most urgent the application of the new popular power to the economic problem. We also find suggested in this statement the explanation of the fact that although democracy in politics was established in America a century before it began to make serious progress in Europe, yet in the Old World the socialistic idea originated fifty years before it began to stir here. Socialism results spontaneously when a people having a pressing economic problem to deal with

become masters of the democratic method. In Europe
the problem was already there and had been for ages,
when the method first came to hand. In America we had
the method of solution but lacked, until recently, any
pressing economic problem to solve. Now the problem
has come, and the Kansas farmer and the New England
wage-earner, as they bring to its solution the democratic
methods they have so long used for other purposes, become in a day socialists, without having ever before heard
of socialism.

Up to within a recent period, owing to our scanty population and vast resources, the question of a comfortable
subsistence has been in America one which every tolerably energetic person has been fairly well able to solve
for himself. So great has been the plenty, that the individualistic, every-man-for-himself-and-the-devil-for-
the-hindmost way of getting a living—crude, wasteful,
brutal as it was—nevertheless sufficed to secure a good
degree of general comfort and an approximate equality
of fortunes. This period has now come to an end. Within the past few decades, the concentration of wealth in
the hands of a few has been proceeding at a rate, ever
growing swifter, which now threatens a practical expropriation of the people in the interest of a small class. Indeed, it may almost be said that this expropriation has
already been practically accomplished, for it has been
shown by direct deductions from the mortgage statistics
of the 1890 census, that seventy-one per cent of the aggregate wealth of the nation is already held by nine per
cent. of the population, the remaining ninety-one per cent.
of the population being limited to twenty-nine per cent.

of the total wealth. It is further shown that 4,074 American families out of a total of 13,000,000 families, own twenty per cent of this national wealth total, or two-thirds as much as belong to the ninety-one per cent. of the population mentioned above.

With such facts and figures to justify his growing sense of economic distress and oppression, the American must indeed be of sluggish mind, who does not recognize already preparing for him, and in course of being fitted to his shoulders, the yoke of economic servitude his European brothers so long have borne. When we reflect that the population thus suddenly and unmistakably confronted with the prospect of degradation to servile and proletarian conditions is the proudest-spirited, the most generally intelligent ever known, with the sentiment of equality bred in the very bones, shall we wonder at the suddenness of the socialistic outburst in the United States, or the swift movement of its propaganda? Must we not rather recognize in the American situation conditions which justify the belief that the suddenness and swiftness of the rise of socialism in this country presage a lusty vigor of growth which shall put America in her proper place as the world's pioneer in the pursuit of economic, as formerly of political, equality? May we not reasonably expect that the American people, having been confronted with the failure of the present economic system to secure human welfare even under the most favorable conditions, will display in the reconstruction of the economic fabric all that energy, that ingenuity and originality of device, and that rapidity of execution which are the distinguishing national characteristics?

# INTRODUCTION TO THE "FABIAN ESSAYS"

Meanwhile, owing to the fact that, for the reasons stated, the social economic problem came earlier to the front in Europe than here, Americans have the advantage of a considerable body of foreign literature, German, French and English, devoted to the subject. Perhaps there is no single work in this socialistic library which is calculated to be more useful to the American reader who desires to obtain without laborious research a general knowledge of the argument for socialism than the "Fabian Essays." This is partly because of their popular style; partly from the excellent arrangement of the matter, with a view to giving an all-around idea of the subject, respectively from the historic, economic and moral view-points; and also in part from the degree of resemblance which obtains between English and American institutions and habits of thought. The fact that the essays are by different authors, each writing in a different style, has an effect to impart a pleasing variety, while the system with which the essays have been grouped secures an effect of coherency and method as satisfactory as could well have been gained by a single authorship. The arrangement of the contents has the further advantage, greatly assisted by the admirable index, of enabling the reader who does not care to read a book in course to select particular topics for study as his interest may incline. It is a pleasure especially to commend the good-tempered and reasonable tone which marks the argument of these writers. This method it is needless to say, far from implying any compromising of the truth, lends itself to a more clear and incisive criticism of existing institutions than is consistent with violent and denuncia-

235

tory rhetoric. The use of this argumentative method which may be described as *suaviter in modo fortiter in re,* is indeed as characteristic of the Fabian Society in England as of the nationalists in the United States.

But it may be that some reader may not know what this Fabian Society exactly is, which gives its name to this volume, and of which the essayists all are members. For the information of any such it may be said that the name was assumed a number of years ago by an organization of cultured Englishmen who, while devoted to a radical socialistic propaganda, believed that they could most effectually promote it by educational methods addressed to the reason rather than the prejudices of the community. In this view they have since been carrying on in England a very extensive and effective work, through tracts, books and, above all, popular lectures, the essays in this volume being indeed but specimens of these popular lectures revised for publication. While the more revolutionary English socialists make a show of deriding as too merely academic the propaganda of the Fabians, it may be doubted if work more valuable has ever been done by any socialist organization.

In addition to the essays contained in the English edition, the present volume includes a valuable and important additional feature in the form of a lecture on "The Fabian Society and Its Work," delivered in Boston by Mr. William Clarke, M. A., himself a Fabian and one of these essayists, in the winter of 1893-94, and afterwards published in the "New England Magazine."

Nationalism is the form under which socialism has thus far been chiefly brought to the notice of the American people; and it is proper in a preface of this character to say a few words by way of explaining the relative significance of the terms, A socialist is one who believes that industry and commerce, on which the welfare of all depend, should not be left as now, to be controlled irresponsibly by individuals for their private gain, but should be organized by the community, to be cooperatively conducted, with an equitable (not necessarily equal) distribution of the product among the members of the community. That is what socialism strictly means, and is all the creed that a socialist can be held to. Now it is a great deal to be able to subscribe to this creed, but it is not quite enough of a creed according to nationalists. The criticism of the present system involved in it is adequate; but in defining the system of cooperation that is to take its place, it leaves unsettled the most vital point of that or any other industrial system, namely, the principle on which the industrial product is to be shared, for to say that the principle of the division is to be "equitable" is no more than to say it should be reasonable, and leaves the whole question open to discussion. There is no standard to determine what an equitable division of anything is, if once we admit it may be an unequal division. The political economists, indeed, argue that the present division of wages and profits is really equitable, although so unequal. Now nationalists are socialists who, holding all that socialists agree on, go further, and hold also that the distribution of the cooperative product among the members of the community must be not merely equitable, whatever that term may mean, but must be always and absolutely equal.

# EDWARD BELLAMY SPEAKS AGAIN!

Of course it is not meant that many socialists are not believers in economic equality, but only that the creed of socialism does not of necessity imply it. Among the essayists in the present volume, Mrs. Besant, and probably others, seem strongly inclined toward the principle of equality, but that cannot be said, hitherto, of the general body of European socialists. The more general opinion among them appears to be that the ownership of the means of production should indeed be communal, but that the product should be apportioned among the workers in the same and in different occupations according to the relative value of their services, as if that could ever be satisfactorily or even practically adjusted under a non-competitive system.

This would leave the individual, as now, to be well-to-do or to want, according to his strength or weakness, and keep alive, although in much less glaring contrast, the economic distinctions of this day. Nationalists, on the other hand, would absolutely abolish these distinctions and the possibility of their again arising, by making an equal provision for the maintenance of all an incident and an indefeasible condition of citizenship, without any regard whatever to the relative specific services of different citizens. The rendering of such services, on the other hand, instead of being left to the option of the citizen with the alternative of starvation, would be required under a uniform law as a civic duty, precisely like other forms of taxation or military service, levied on the citizen for the furtherance of a common-weal in which each is to share equally. This is called nationalism, not in any narrow tribal sense opposed to universal fraternity, but because it consists in applying to the economic organization the idea exemplified in all national or public functions when undertaken in democratic or even in the progressive class of monarchical States.

All such public functions are supported either by tax or personal service, of the citizens, or both. The obligation of that service of tax or person is enforced by a uniform levy, but the amount of tax or service rendered under that levy is very unequal, depending on ability. This inequality of service is not, however, allowed to prejudice the right of all citizens to claim an equal benefit from all national or public expenditure or action. The rule of the State in coordinating the efforts of its members for any public purpose is the equal distribution of benefits resulting from necessarily unequal but uniformly levied contributions. So it must be when the nation assumes the organization of industry. The law of service must be uniform, but the services rendered will vary greatly—with many entire exemptions—according to the abilities of the people. The inequality of contributions will in no way prejudice the invariable law of equal distribution of the resultant sum.

It is confidently believed that all socialists will ultimately be led by the logic of events to recognize, as many now do, that the attitude of the nationalists on this point is the only true socialistic one.

# Is the Prophet Dead?

### By John Clark Ridpath

*(Editor, The Arena, August 1898)*

A MAN curious to inquire into the secret things sat one evening at a seance. There was what seemed to be a materialization. After several questions had been propounded and as many answers given, the Man said to the Spirit, "Are you going away?" "No," said the Spirit; "not going away, but disappearing."

When a prophet dies he does not go away; he disappears. The real presence of the departing seer remains behind and expresses itself evermore in his works. It is for this reason that we speak always of the bards and prophets as being still alive. They are always in the present tense. They are so identified with their works that by an easy metonymy we put the book for the man; we say that we read *him* when we read the book; we say, though he be dead, that he *says* so and so, not that he *said* so and so. It would be a queer critic who should refer to anything that Shakespeare *said*.

Edward Bellamy was a prophet. Dying, he did not go away; he only disappeared. Nature must indeed be an unmoral fact to spare a prizefighter and send a consumption after Edward Bellamy. Let us inquire briefly how this prophet should be regarded by his fellow mortals who have not disappeared from the arena of visible life.

241

# EDWARD BELLAMY SPEAKS AGAIN!

In attempting to estimate the career and work of this man, other men are placed in a certain attitude towards him and his work. Whoever has read the two principal productions of Bellamy has taken a certain stand with respect to him and his theory of civilization. In the first place, he who believes in the Existing Order can have no part or lot with Edward Bellamy. He who does not believe in the Existing Order, but fears to disturb it, has no part or lot with him either. He who disbelieves in the Existing Order, but who thinks on the whole that it were better to let it alone than to go forward to some new social and economic condition which has not yet been tested and proved by the experience of men, may have something in common with Bellamy, but not much. He who disbelieves in the Existing Order and is willing to patch up the structure with expedients and makeshifts, eking out a little here and plastering a little there, may have vaguely before him the same end which Bellamy sought to reach; but he does not have Bellamy's method, his inspiration, or his hope. He who disbelieves in the Existing Order—who puts it from him roughly in the insurgent spirit and with revolutionary methods—who hews and hacks little regardful of what he scars or where his splinters may fall, has Bellamy's objects in view, but he does not have his spirit or his method.

Edward Bellamy was on the whole one of the gentlest and most humane revolutionists that ever lived. He was so mild-mannered in his innovations, so peaceable in thought and life, so sympathetic even with the distorted conditions of human society, that we scarcely know how to classify him. Was he really a rebel, an insur-

rectionist? Certainly he carried neither axe nor torch.
Certainly he contemplated no such revolution as that
which once set ablaze in a single fortnight hundreds of
chateaux all over France. Certain Bellamy did not wish
to carry any rough and bloody reform with sword and
vomiting cannon—carry it in such manner as to drive
forth from their luxurious strongholds of ease and greed
the idle nobility of our American empire. Bellamy
sought not to squeeze out any—not to set thirty thousand
emigrants a-flying across continents and seas—but rather
to squeeze in many; to give the millions a chance; to set
the weak and the fallen on their feet again; and this to
the end that individuality under a sort of public socialism may to this extent assert itself, that in the final as-
sizes every human being shall attain to "the dignity of
the unit and count one."

It is very far from my purpose to trace the course of
Edward Bellamy's life, or to enter into a critical analysis
and estimate of his two great books. They are with us;
he is gone. They remain to speak to us of the purpose
of his life and the nature of his philosophy when he himself is as far away as Gautama and the generations of
Japheth. What I have to say of him and his work relates only to his general attitude with respect to human
society, such as it is at the close of the nineteenth century.

Bellamy being an American, lived to see with most
penetrating vision the evil conditions into which we have
come. He lived to discern this, that the abuse of prop
erty and of property rights under organization is the

origin of the greater part of the unhappiness of the modern world. He perceived most clearly that it is not original sin, but aboriginal robbery that has undone mankind. He clearly perceived the difference between the book-made, traditional sin against which the theologians are wont to thunder, and that deep-rooted, awful human harm which undoes the world and leaves the fairest hopes prostrate in the dust.

In considering this dreadful harm, done by man to man, by man to society, and by society to the individual, Bellamy discovered that nearly all of it has its root in the property condition, or, as we have said, in the abuse of property rights under organization. He therefore studied profoundly the state of inequality in society, diagnosed our diseases, and in his higher moods went so far as to suggest certain practical remedies by which a reform, as he thought, might be carried in every civilized nation. No doubt he began with the fact that in the first stages of social development the individual acts for himself and by himself in the acquisition of property. He saw that the next stage of the economic evolution introduces the principle and fact of association, or copartnership. In this stage men associate together in order to do and to have what they cannot do and save singly, or individually.

To this day the individual acquisition and possession of property continues. To get property is now the bottom motive in the struggle for existence. Occasionally we still find a rich miser in his seclusion, who, acting silently by individual methods, has amassed a fortune, and at

244

the same time by self-denial has brought himself into moral atrophy, intellectual paralysis, and bodily ossification.  Copartnership also survives in the business world, and its methods are still known and employed by men in association; but this form of association is weakened; it gives place at length to the corporation, which is the third stage in the economic evolution.  Of the corporation we have had in our times ample and baleful demonstration.  We have seen it rise on the ruins of partnership.  We have seen it attack civil society and compel that society to give it the right to flourish and to reign.

But beyond the corporation there arises a still greater and more abusive fact, and that is the trust.  Edward Bellamy saw the trust rising above the corporate life and drawing into its own circle of power, not one corporation, but hundreds and thousands of them, making them the materials of its own life.

It is at this point that modern society has made a pause.  Bellamy, however, perceived that the pause is only temporary.  He perceived clearly that there is no finality in the human evolution, but only an ongoing and new development for ever and ever.  He therefore looked ahead and anticipated somewhat the possible state of society to come.  He looked beyond the corporation and the trust, beyond the prodigious development of modern commercialism and municipality, and saw something higher and grander than these rising in the distance.  What he saw towering in dim outline was the Social Trust of which all men are to be the beneficiaries.  He imagined the possibility of seizing upon the present order and converting its gigantic evils by a gentle curve into the way of the greatest good. He saw beyond the existing order arising in dim outline the COOPERA- TIVE COMMONWEALTH—a sort of socio-industrial, intellectual, and moral commune of associated interest, of mutual support and counsel.

It was at this point that Bellamy made his splendid leap. In doing so he was perfectly rational. He knew that society is not going to stop at its present stage of development. He knew that something else besides the present order must arise and stand in its stead. Dis- believing in the present order, he attempted in an ideal way, very gently and humanely to put the present order aside. His effort was made with the pen. It was made in right reason and with the virtue of a great moral pur- pose. It was made in a manner so interesting as to draw the sympathetic attention of the whole world to this weak-bodied but great-souled man. The common folk among the nations took up his first book and saw reflected in it something of their own dreams and hopes. The leaders of society took it up, followed the argument, and admitted its truthfulness so far as the disease and the diagnosis are concerned, but refused to follow fur- ther. After their manner they yawned and laid down the volume. Indeed it may be said in a general way that all of Bellamy has been accepted except his remedial agencies and his prophetic indications.

This is the manner, however, of the English-speaking race. The man who speaks English never accepts any- thing until it is thrust upon him. Generally he does not accept it until it is forced upon him by revolution.

# IS THE PROPHET DEAD?

Afterward he will say that he likes it very much and that he was always striving to get it. There is a strange admixture of cowardice and courage, of daring and conservatism, of reformatory tendency and stolid reactionism in the Anglo-Saxon constitution. If the race were practically as adventurous in the direction of ideal betterment as it is in the way of geographical adventure, sea-faring, conquest, colonization, and government, then by the agency of this courageous but immobile division of mankind the world would long ere this have reached a millennium.

But the English-speaking people hold back from any rapid approach toward ideal conditions. The whole product, therefore, of civilization which the Anglo-Saxon stock has produced is essentially like an old English cathedral, which, beginning in a shanty, has never demolished anything, but always added to it and covered it up; and to this day should anyone search in the heart or remote wing of the cathedral for the original hut, and should he propose to remove it with its rat-holes and bat-haunts, the whole race would be up in arms for fear the Existing Order might be disturbed, religion injured, and society be visited with the vengeance of heaven on the score of sacrilege.

Had we the courage to clear away sometimes, to lay a new foundation, to bring in a new architecture that shall be consistent with itself and equal to the aspiration of the age, then we should all become apostles of Edward Bellamy. In that event we should take up and carry forward, if not complete, the building of that exquisite

and humane structure which the author of "Looking
Backward" and "Equality" beheld in his visions and
dreams.

## THE END

The hope of truth grows stronger day by day.
I hear the soul of man around me waking,
Like a great sea, its frozen fetters breaking,
And flinging up to heaven its sunlit spray;
Tossing huge continents in scornful play
And crushing them with din of grinding thunder,
That makes old emptiness stare in wonder;
The memory of a glory passed away
Lingers in every heart, as in the shell
Resounds the by-gone freedom of the sea,
And every hour new signs of promise tell
That the great soul shall once again be free;
For high and yet more high the murmurs swell
Of inward strife for truth and liberty.

JAMES RUSSELL LOWELL.